Stop Bringing

Them to Church

Who the Church Is, Isn't, and Why We Should Keep It That Way

David Washington

BHF Publishing

3628 Torrance Dr.

Toledo, Ohio 43612-0639

Website: bereanhomechurch.org

Email: bhf@bereanhomechurch.org

Unless otherwise noted, scripture quotations are taken from the King
James Version of the Bible.

ISBN 10: 0615832091

ISBN 13: 978-0615832098

To the Lord Jesus Christ for creating me, saving me, and gifting me, all for His glory.

To my wife who has been my best friend and stalwart supporter in my writing endeavors and just as a wife. I'm a truly blessed man to have you as my soul mate.

To my church and for your patience and indulgence with me.

To my teachers who have unknowingly poured fountains of knowledge and wisdom into my life and continue to do so.

To my alpha readers. Thank you for your investment of time into this . You are a blessing and of high value to me.

To those who disagree. You spur me on to plumb the depths of the scriptures even more.

I am thankful for you all. I love you all.

Table of Contents

Introduction

This book was written out of a necessity. Like Jeremiah, the words were like fire shut up in my bones. They had to be released. I was compelled to write it as I was reading the word of God and it kept presenting itself before me.

It all started in a series of articles I had written back in 2010. I received some criticism as well as some encouragement in dealing with the subject matter which has all but disappeared into the ether in this age of fast food, feel good, non-Christianity posing as Christianity.

I will be the first to admit that the administering of new methods for a cultural or even social subset in reference to the gospel is a biblical mandate. Paul laid this out rather plainly in his first letter to the Corinthians when he stated:

> *For though I be free from all men, yet have I made myself servant unto all, that I might gain the more. And unto the Jews I became as a Jew, that I might gain the Jews; to them that are under the law, as under the law, that I might gain them that are under the law; To them that are without law, as without law, (being not without law to God, but under the law to Christ,) that I might gain them that are without law. To the weak became I as weak, that I might gain the weak: I am made all things to all men, that I might by all*

means save some. (1 Corinthians 9:19-22)

Some have taken that scripture, distorted it, and run far afield. If we are to obey it, we are to do so without compromise to the gospel of grace or the word of God in general.

As God's people, there are times where we have to sit back and ask why are we doing the things we are doing. This book is written as an attempt to answer several questions the church should be asking but appear to be totally ignoring: Who and/or what is the biblical church? Who is a part of that church? Who are we bringing to the church? Why do we bring people to church? Should we bring them to the church? Lastly and most importantly, what does the Bible have to say about all of this? The answers to these questions may surprise you. They surprised me and gave me a whole different outlook on the church which simultaneously increased my appreciation for the church as never before. It also forced me to shift my thinking not to the whims of the church culture and tradition, but to the truth of it as it is laid out in the scriptures. It was an experience that challenged me to conform to the word of God. My hope is that it does the same for you as well.

In order to answer these questions thoroughly and accurately, we must delve into God's word first and foremost. I quote a plethora of scripture because as a Christian I believe in its authority, sufficiency, and power. It is the bedrock foundation that the church and much of what is identified as Christianity has relegated to an inferior position. In its place are sand-built programs, stories, self-help advice, and methods that run counter to what scripture commands us to teach and does not have the support of truth and therefore God Himself.

Paradigm shifts are not comfortable, especially when tradition has entrenched itself firmly and refuses to budge. Within these pages are the kinds of things that will get one labeled a rebel, heretic, and in the extreme cases, make people want to kill you. Now, I don't believe anyone will want to kill me over this book (fingers crossed). My intent is not to go out and write something that's going to make a whole lot of people upset and angry. But I know it will for truth does that. It's its nature. Novelist, satirist, and self-proclaimed agnostic Aldous Huxley nailed it when he said:

You shall know the truth, and the truth will make you mad.

It is my hope that this small work may challenge us all to think more biblically and act more bravely in this cultural climate. This is a time when the edicts, commands, laws, and tenets of the scriptures are whittled down into powerless sound-bites for fast consumption by a society that is becoming more and more indifferent to the word of God, God Himself, or altogether ignored. Nowhere is this more prevalent than among the visible church.

This book is now released but I cannot say it is "finished". As

I let the book sit for a while, the Lord kept showing me more and more in His word where He spoke of this throughout all of scripture - more than what is covered in these pages. So, I would ask that you would consider this a primer or beginning. A revision is inevitable.

My hope is that this small work will become a part of the clarion call to those who would listen, and to have our minds renewed to conform to His word in all things so that whether we eat or drink, we do it unto the glory of God.

-David Washington

Chapter 1

The Church: What It Is Not

"We must cease to think of the church as a gathering of institutions and organizations, and we must get back to the notion that we are the people of God." - Martyn Lloyd Jones

IN A WORLD where the church often redefines itself as well as its theology, pinpointing what the church is has become somewhat of a challenge and, more often than not, a confusing endeavor. So we must start at the beginning and seek a biblical definition of the church, starting with what it is not.

It's Not a Building

For most, the church is still identified by the building that the congregants meet in when in fact that's not the case at all. This misconception has been going on since the advent of the church building. Having a church building is not to blame for this kind of erroneous thinking as much as a lack of solid biblical teaching or understanding on the matter.

The first mention of the church in the scriptures is in Matthew 16:18. The Lord declares after Peter had announced the revelation of who He was:

And I say also unto thee, that thou art Peter, and upon this rock I will build My church, and the gates of hell shall not prevail against it.

The word "church" is translated from the Greek word *ekklesia* which literally means "called out ones." It speaks of the people, not the building. The building, known as a sanctuary or temple, was not known among Christians until centuries later. They were used to meeting in homes, camps, along the roads, catacombs, and wherever it was convenient with homes being the most popular. Frank C. Senn, author of *Christian Liturgy: Catholic and Evangelical,* notes:

> Christians of the first several centuries lacked the publicity of the pagan cults. They had no shrines, temples, statues, or sacrifices. They staged no public festivals, dances, musical performances, or pilgrimages. Their central ritual involved a meal

(Lord's table) that had a domestic origin and setting inherited from Judaism. Indeed, Christians of the first three centuries usually met in private residences that had been converted into suitable gathering spaces for the Christian community. [1]

Though this may seem like splitting hairs to some, I beg to differ. These details are important especially if we are to recapture what the church really is in a culture that defines it by something else other than its true biblical definition.

It's Not a Social Club

Sunday mornings have a lot of similarities for many churches around the world. At the beginning, there's a time for greeting and smiles. Some come dressed in three-piece suits and dresses. Others come in khakis and a polo shirt. Still others come in jeans and a t-shirt.

The formal niceties complete, there's a time of musical worship. This again may be different. For some it may be a choir while for others it's a full band. The first song is usually a mid to fast tempo It's time to praise the Lord.

After a few songs, the tempo slows down and the music gets more contemplative. The songs are meant to draw us into an intimate encounter with the Lord. Hands are lifted throughout the sanctuary while others bow their heads. It all ends on a rather solemn tone.

After this, there may be some announcements updating the members about events and other happenings among the church. Then there's the sermon. There may be a scripture reference, a story or some illustrations (more and more the Bible is not part of the central focus of a church gathering which is simply ludicrous...but I digress). Some feel that the message was just for them. Others learn something new. They have something to think about. As the sermon ends, some music may begin to play, the benediction is read, and the church is dismissed.

Even if what the church is and what it stands for is understood, there's still a mindset that it's a social club of some sort and that the preceding description is simply meeting protocol. In order to be a part of the club, you must act a certain way, dress in specific clothing, and have an air of piety. For far too many, it's a time to watch a musical performance instead of entering into worship of the Most High God of the universe. Some use the time for business endeavors, not really listening to the sermon or concerned about its application to their lives. They're waiting for it all to be over to see who they can talk with about becoming their latest client. Others use it as a time for sin, gossiping about others who may be in the church or their neighborhood. Ungodly cliques form reminiscent of high school except adults are the ones creating them and there's competition on who will be the most influential or well liked.

In other words, the focus is everything but God.

Though the church is social because it's a community, what this particular community does (and should do) is not concentrated on being a social event to hang out with friends and acquaintances. The church is not an organization. It's an organism. It's not about the pastor, elders, lay people, music, or the building. It should be centered around the Lord Jesus Christ, the Son of the Living God through the truth of His word.

It's Not Something We Do

You might see it on television as a pastor preaches in the midst of a stirring sermon or during a moving gospel song. You can feel the excitement building and the energy is climbing as the music gets louder and people are shouting. Then, at the climax of it all, the pastor shouts, "Alright! Now we're having church!"

Uh...what?

The church is not an event. This kind of vulgarizing of the church demeans it to something that we do instead of something that we are. It misrepresents the whole idea of what the church is supposed to be. When presented in this way, people begin to identify a church gathering with how loud the music is and how excited everyone in the sanctuary can be. It's as if to say the only way to have a truly spiritual experience is to pump up the volume and be extremely emotional. It is a shameful way of presenting the church to an unbelieving world.

This is not to say that the church can't be emotional in its gathering. Far from that. There are churches that stifle the expression of emotion all for the sake of order or under some misguided misinterpretation of the scriptures by equating it with a lack of self control which ultimately ends up quenching the Spirit. That's not what I'm advocating. What I'm saying is that when we *define* the church as such we are presenting it erroneously and are not truly focusing on the main thing which is *being* the church.

To some, this may be stretching the canvass and semantic nitpicking when it comes to the freedom of the church but I beg to differ. Throughout the pages of scripture, the focus is not on an event but on a Being. Next to that is on conforming to the image of that Being. The last thing we need in this day and age are more confusing terms that lose an already confused world about who and what the church is. We need to cease misrepresenting the church not only in our actions but also in our speech where it starts.

We'll now expand the definition by taking a look at who and what is the true, biblical church.

References

1. Christian Liturgy: Catholic and Evangelical, Frank. C Senn, pg. 53

Chapter 2

The Church: What It Is

"The church is the community of all true believers for all time. This definition understands the church to be made of all those who are truly saved ." - Wayne Grudem

"The word 'church' in Scripture has always one meaning, and one only: an assembly of the people of God, a society of Christians." - Thomas Witherow

HAVING DEFINED WHAT the church is not, we can now answer the question, "What is the church?" To discover this, we must go to the scriptures.

In short, the church is the people of God, the body of Christ, and covenant community.

The People of God

The church is presented in the scriptures as God's people and are referred to multiple times as saints:

Paul, an apostle of Jesus Christ by the will of God, and Timotheus our brother, to the saints and faithful brethren in Christ which are at Colosse: Grace be unto you, and peace, from God our Father and the Lord Jesus Christ. (Colossians 1:1-2)

To all that be in Rome, beloved of God, called to be saints: Grace to you and peace from God our Father, and the Lord Jesus Christ. (Romans 1:7)

The word saint is translated from the Greek word *hagios* which means "sacred" or "holy one." As can be seen in the apostle Paul's greeting, he addressed all those in the churches as saints. Later, the early Roman Catholic church began to identify saints as those who were martyred for their faith. These people were accorded special honor and even worshiped (the latter being a *big* no, no, since this is idolatry). The term "saint" stuck and today it has been used inaccurately to refer to only these special individuals, primarily in the Catholic church, giving special qualifications as to who is considered a saint through passing certain requirements (like the working of a specific amount of miracles).

Throughout the New Testament, saints are synonymous with

those who are the true followers of Christ. Period. I am a saint and there are many I know who are saints as well. These are those who have heard the glorious gospel of grace and respond positively, exhibiting the two marks of a true saint.

Repentance

The Lord was very clear on the precursor to a true saving faith:

...but except you repent, you shall likewise perish. (Luke 13:3)

Not only did He say that but it was proclaimed by his predecessor, John the Baptist:

In those days came John the Baptist, preaching in the wilderness of Judaea, And saying, Repent ye: for the kingdom of heaven is at hand. (Matthew 3:1-2)

And after the Lord, the apostles preached the same:

Then Peter said unto them, Repent, and be baptized every one of you in the name of Jesus Christ for the remission of sins, and ye shall receive the gift of the Holy Ghost. (Acts 2:38)

But shewed first unto them of Damascus, and at Jerusalem, and throughout all the coasts of Judaea, and then to the Gentiles, that they should repent and turn to God, and do works meet for repentance. (Acts 26:20)

The word repent is translated from the Greek word *metanoeo* which means "to think differently or reconsider." Pastor and writer Clark Palmer explains:

> In its biblical sense repentance refers to a deeply seated
> and thorough turning from self to God…[The] complete
> redirection of their lives was to be demonstrated by pro-
> found changes in lifestyle and relationships...the call
> to repentance is a call to absolute surrender to the purposes
> of God and to live in this awareness.[1]

The Lord Jesus considered this to be the cornerstone of His ministry:

I came not to call the righteous, but sinners to repentance. (Luke 5:32)

This repentance is seen as an outworking of the Holy Spirit. He empowers the believer to believe in accordance with the word of God, which is expressed through holy living and a desire and joy in the things of God. This is the precursor to being a Christian. Not being a church-goer. Not being baptized. Not being raised in a "Christian" home (which is often not the case when people say that). It is repentance. Without it, a person is not saved which makes that person not a Christian.

Continuance

The second mark of a true saint is continuance in the faith. The apostle John made this distinction in 1 John 2:19:

They went out from us, but they were not of us; for if they had been of us, they would no doubt have continued with us: but they went out, that they might be made manifest that they were not all of us.

John repeats this idea a few verses later:

Let that therefore abide in you, which ye have heard from the beginning. If that which ye have heard from the beginning shall remain in you, ye also shall continue in the Son, and in the Father. (1 John 1:24)

The implication here is that there were some that walked for a while but ended up falling away. John says even though they were with them for a time, they really were never a part of them, meaning the church. They never were saints. They never were Christians.

I must interject here with a small note that there is no such thing as someone who used to be saved or used to be a Christian. It is once saved, always saved. If someone falls away, it simply means they were never saved. The Lord makes this clear in John 6:39:

*And this is the Father's will which hath sent me, that of all which he hath given me **I should lose nothing** (emphasis mine), but should raise it up again at the last day.*

However, that is a subject that should be presented in another book in its entirety.

Paul also presents continuance as the litmus test of a true saint:

Take heed unto thyself, and unto the doctrine; continue in them: for in doing this thou shalt both save thyself, and them that hear thee. (1 Timothy 4:16)

And you, that were sometime alienated and enemies in your mind by wicked works, yet now hath he reconciled. In the body of his flesh through death, to present you holy and unblameable and unreproveable in his sight: If ye continue in the faith grounded and settled, and be not moved away from the hope of the gospel, which ye have heard, and which was preached to every creature which is under heaven; whereof I Paul am made a minister. (Colossians 1:21-23)

In the book of Hebrews, there is a blessed and specific place for the believer. We are citizens of the heavenly Mount Zion and have our names written in the Book of Life. This gives us citizenship in heaven now, by faith, as we live here on earth (Hebrew 12:22-23). Only those who are truly saved, having repented of their sins and continue in the faith can claim membership in the church of Christ, the household of God.

Why is this important? Because it goes to the heart of what the true church is supposed to be and of whom it's comprised. Granted, there is no flawless church while we're here on earth but the prerequisite for anyone to become a part of the church is that they are truly followers of the Lord Jesus Christ. This means there is strong affirmative evidence of a changed life, growth in holiness, and a closer walk with the Lord Jesus. It should be apparent to those watching us that we are who 1 Peter 2:9 says we are:

But ye are a chosen generation, a royal priesthood, an holy nation, a peculiar people; that ye should shew forth the praises of him who hath called you out of darkness into his marvelous light:

Body of Christ

One of the unique monikers given to the church of Christ is that we are a body.

Now ye are the body of Christ, and members in particular. (1 Corinthians 12:27)

Christians all around the world share an interconnectedness that is special and exclusive only to those who are followers of the Lord. Each part is needed for its specific function as we carry out the tasks assigned to us through the Head, who is Christ (Ephesians 1:21-23). It is a foregone conclusion that we are part of the body of Christ once we come into faith. That is to say that those who are His are automatically a part of the body of Christ. This means we're supposed to be an extension of who He is. We can do this because we are living as saints, operating through the power of the Holy Spirit, reflecting His holiness and beauty in our lives.

Christian Wolf in the *Holman Bible Dictionary* notes:

> The individual Christian is joined to Christ only as a member of the body [of Christ]. The Bible knows nothing of a direct, mythical union of the individual with the Lord. The Bible knows of a union with Christ only as faith embodied in the realm of the church community and with the church in the realm of the world.[2]

Dr. John MacArthur explains:

> There is one body in which all function yet never do
> they lose their personal identity and the essential
> necessity of ministry as God has designed them to
> do it.[3]

There's not only an interconnectedness between those who are in the body of Christ, but there's also an interdependence. Paul expresses this interdependence in 1 Corinthians 12:21-25. This means no one is a Lone Ranger. An eye can't survive on its own and neither can an ear, nose, mouth, or any other part of the body. It's only when they are working in concert and unity that the body functions as it should effectively as the Head is leads and guides everything.

Covenant Community

Christian fellowship is an exclusive relationship between Christian believers. It is the body of Christ in operation.

Bradley Chance, professor of Religion at William Jewell College, defines fellowship as the following:

> Bond of common purpose and devotion that binds
> Christians to one another and to Christ. "Fellow-
> ship" is the English translation from the Hebrew
> stem *chabar* and the Greek stem *koin*. The Hebrew
> *chabar* was used to express ideas such as common
> or shared house...Paul believed that Christians

were to share with one another what they had to offer to assist fellow believers. Paul used the *koin* stem to refer to such sharing...Paul actually used the term *koinonia* to denote the financial contribution which he was collecting from Gentile believers to take to Jerusalem for the relief of the saints who lived there.[4]

When the church says fellowship today, we often mean a time for eating (overeating normally) while everyone just relaxes in a social, church environment. That's not true fellowship.

Fellowship in the New Testament goes deeper, reflecting a depth of love that looks out for the well being of other Christians. It could be expressed in a number of ways: financially, practically, and emotionally, as well as spiritually. This commonality extends to all areas of our lives. We see this exemplified in the first church:

And all that believed were together, and had all things common; And sold their possessions and goods, and parted them to all men, as every man had need. And they, continuing daily with one accord in the temple, and breaking bread from house to house, did eat their meat with gladness and singleness of heart, praising God, and having favor with all the people. And the Lord added to the church daily such as should be saved. (Acts 2:44-47)

An important detail to note in the previous Acts passage is

that it was not a once -a-week event but an every day reality. The tie that binds Christians is truly eternal and much more serious than we take it, especially in the American church. Christians help and aid other Christians because they are a part of the family of God. This is alluded to in the book of Galatians:

And let us not be weary in well doing: for in due season we shall reap, if we faint not. As we have therefore opportunity, let us do good unto all men, especially unto them who are of the household of faith. (Galatians 6:9-10)

In the book of Ephesians, it is reiterated that those who are believers are of the household of God:

Now therefore ye are no more strangers and foreigners, but fellow citizens with the saints, and of the household of God; (Ephesians 2:19)

Because of this special place a believer holds within the household of God, the church is to be given priority. This doesn't give us a license to ignore our family responsibilities or absolve us from taking care of an unbeliever who has needs when we're able to help. Every situation will be different and we should be wise as serpents and harmless as doves when evaluating each circumstance. However, it does mean that we give a special consideration to God's family first. Hands down. In a nutshell, it means the church should have a special emphasis in taking care of its own.

The Lord Jesus said that His children, His people, are of paramount concern to Him.

But whoso shall offend one of these little ones which believe in me, it were better for him that a millstone were hanged about his neck, and that he were drowned in the depth of the sea. (Matthew 18:6)

What the Lord is saying is that it would be better that someone would suffer a horrible death then to cause one of His own to sin. He is gravely serious about His saints and we should be equally as serious about belonging to His family and about others who are in the family of God. You would think that by the way many professing Christians treat one another that they are more enemies than brothers and sisters. But the call for the people of God is clear and consistent:

By this shall all men know that ye are my disciples, if ye have love to one another. (John 13:35)

Be kindly affectioned one to another with brotherly love; in honour preferring one another; (Romans 12:10)

But as touching brotherly love ye need not that I write unto you: for ye yourselves are taught of God to love one another. (1 Thessalonians 4:9)

The conduct of covenant community is serious. We are exhorted to encourage one another to good works (Hebrews 10:24), to bear each other's burdens (Galatians 6:2), not to cause one another to stumble into sin (Romans 14:3), and to provide for each others' needs (Galatians 6:10). We are constantly in service to God, one another and the world. We should be protective of the family of God as well as elated to be a part of God's eternal household, recognizing it as the high privilege it is.

Know Thyself

Some may be wondering why the long dissertation on the church's identity. Quite simple: if you don't know who you are, then you certainly won't know how you should be. The church has lost its identity from a biblical standpoint and this has caused a schism on many levels. Whether it be denominationalism (which is simply another form of sectarianism), personal dislike toward members of other churches which normally leads to gossip, slander, and envy, or simply indifference to other churches, we need to understand that we are all in this together. We should be in the business of promoting unity and love within the household of God as well as other spiritual duties and responsibilities, which I will lay out later.

Once we are firmly aware of who we are supposed to be, we can pursue our purpose in the right way and for the right reasons. We'll begin to take a look at those purposes in the next chapter.

References

1. Holman Bible Dictionary, Clark Palmer, page 1376.

2. Holman Bible Dictionary, Chris Wolf, pg 229

3. The MacArthur Bible Commentary, John MacArthur, pg. 1595

4. Holman Bible Dictionary, Bradley Chance, pg. 563-564

Chapter 3

The Ultimate Purpose of the Church

"Man's chief end is to glorify God and to enjoy Him forever." - Westminster Shorter Catechism

SUNDAY AFTER SUNDAY, many people gather with their local church thinking that the long and the short of church life happens on Sunday. They are ignorant of what they are a part of and what, if any, their role is in all of it. For most, they are under the impression that the church is only there to serve them. While a church does have a responsibility to serve those within it, it's not the ultimate purpose of the church. So if gathering on Sunday isn't the main purpose of the church, what is its purpose? There is one main reason for the existence of the church—it is to glorify God.

Glorify God

The primary and fundamental purpose of the church in its entirety is to glorify God.

I will say to the north, Give up; and to the south, Keep not back: bring my sons from far, and my daughters from the ends of the earth; Even every one that is called by my name: for I have created him for my glory, I have formed him; yea, I have made him. (Isaiah 43:6-7)

Now the God of patience and consolation grant you to be likeminded one toward another according to Christ Jesus: That ye may with one mind and one mouth glorify God, even the Father of our Lord Jesus Christ. (Romans 15:5-6)

Whether therefore ye eat, or drink, or whatsoever ye do, do all to the glory of God. (1 Corinthians 10:31)

What exactly does "glorify God" mean? What does it entail? In its most basic sense, to glorify means to esteem greatly or to highly honor. Giving glory to God as the church comes in a number of different ways and includes the aspects that follow it in this list. This list is not meant to be exhaustive. However, I argue that these are pillars of virtue that God expects from His people (which the modern church either dismisses or misconstrues). They need to be elevated back to their proper place. Without them, the church cannot effectively fulfill its ultimate purpose.

Holiness

When asked to think about an attribute of God, many Christians' first response is love, mercy, or goodness. Though He is most definitely all of those things, He puts a premium on one attribute. That is, His holiness. It is an attribute that the church exclusively is called to because the world cannot be holy without being a part of God's people.

In Isaiah 6, the prophet is recounting a vision. There surrounding the throne of God are seraphim, six winged servants of God. Isaiah describes the scene:

Above it stood the seraphims: each one had six wings; with twain he covered his face, and with twain he covered his feet, and with twain he did fly. And one cried unto another, and said, Holy, holy, holy, is the LORD of hosts: the whole earth is full of his glory. (Isaiah 6:2-3)

There is a similar scene in the book of Revelation:

And the four beasts had each of them six wings about him; and they were full of eyes within: and they rest not day and night, saying, Holy, holy, holy, Lord God Almighty, which was, and is, and is to come. (Revelation 4:8)

Out of all the things they could say about the God of the universe, they don't cry, "Loving, loving, loving" or "Good, good, good." They cry "Holy, holy, holy." God uses this term more than any other to describe Himself.

For I am the LORD your God: ye shall therefore sanctify yourselves, and ye shall be holy; for I am holy: (Leviticus 11:44a)

So will I make my holy name known in the midst of my people Israel; and I will not let them pollute my holy name any more: and the heathen shall know that I am the LORD, the Holy One in Israel. (Ezekiel 39:7)

The word "holy" is a term that means "separate from." Another way to look at it is He is "other than" everything else in existence. He is so far separate from everything that the angels in heaven reiterate it over and over. There is none or nothing like Him, neither will there ever be. God is the epitome and personification of holiness. This separation also includes sin. There is no sin in Him and therefore He's the personification of everything that is good. Without God, we would not only cease to exist, but even if it were possible, there would be nothing good in the world.

As God is separate from everything in existence to where He can't be tainted by it and is far different from it, His people, when they reflect this same separateness from the world, glorify Him. It is part of the special calling of the Christian.

But as he which hath called you is holy, so be ye holy in all manner of conversation; (1 Peter 1:15)

The one thing that is sadly apparent in too many modern churches today is the desire to see just how close they can be to the world. This is justified by saying the church should be "relevant" to the culture. However, God did not call us to be relevant. He called us to be faithful. Faithful to His word, to the truth.

To use some man-made scheme to try and lure people to the church is the backward way of doing things. We don't need to market the church. We need to be holy. The more holiness we reflect as the church of God, the more the world will hate us.

If the world hate you, ye know that it hated me before it hated you. If ye were of the world, the world would love his own: but because ye are not of the world, but I have chosen you out of the world, therefore the world hateth you. (John 15:18-19)

Holiness breeds hatred from a world that loves darkness. The Lord Jesus Christ is the epitome of holiness and the world nailed Him to a cross for it. Trying to be accepted by the world is a sure way of being rejected by God because the world is His enemy.

Ye adulterers and adulteresses, know ye not that the friendship of the world is enmity with God? Whosoever therefore will be a friend of the world is the enemy of God. (James 4:4)

In saying this, I must mention that this does not give license for Christians to be judgmental, critical, and hostile towards those who are unbelievers (though we should be hostile towards unbelief). On the contrary, holiness should bring the fruit of the Spirit (Galatians 5:23). Patience, goodness, love, self-control, gentleness and so on. There is no law against such things, so we should seek to foster and build on these to reflect God's glory.

The opposite of holiness, of course, would be to live

unholy which in contrast has the opposite effect in its reflection on God. Instead of glorifying God, it blasphemes (speaks evil of or slanders) His name. It's the equivalent of spitting in God's face.

Righteousness

Righteousness has a meaning on several different levels in the scriptures. In one sense, it's used for certain objects in the Old Testament (Deuteronomy 4:8, 33:19). It's related to sociocovenental justice by the prophets (Isaiah 9:2-7, 60:17). However, righteousness in general is doing what is right or being in a right (correct, positive, good) standing with God. The book of Proverbs gives many character traits that a righteous person will exhibit which include honesty, steadfastness, courage, loving of God and the things of God, and wise.

D. Jefferey Mooney notes in the Holman Bible Dictionary:

…the righteous person is pictured as the quintessential covenant keeper; one committed to God and living justly among his people. [1]

This righteousness is predicated on obeying the word of God in faith. Even in ignorance a person can perform a correct act, but it does not make them righteous because it is not done in faith. It is God and God alone who makes a man truly righteous and He does this based on faith in His Son, Jesus the Christ's, work on the cross and obedience to His word.

And the scripture was fulfilled which saith, Abraham believed God, and it was imputed unto him for righteousness: and he was called the friend of God. (James 2:23)

There's a "righteousness" that is lower, base, and unprofitable for the kingdom of God. This is the righteousness of man which really isn't righteousness at all. Isaiah declares:

But we are all as an unclean thing, and all our righteousnesses are as filthy rags; and we all do fade as a leaf; and our iniquities, like the wind, have taken us away. (Isaiah 64:6)

This is the same kind of righteousness that the Pharisees had. It was a righteousness by works which Paul states is not the true righteousness of God:

For I bear them record that they have a zeal of God, but not according to knowledge. For being ignorant of God's righteousness, and going about to establish their own righteousness, have not submitted themselves to the righteousness of God. (Romans 10:2-3)

We receive the true righteousness of God when we become the children of God through faith in Christ. We then exhibit this righteousness by obeying the word of God. This means we stand for what is right not according to the dictates of the world, but according to the word of the Living God.

And have no fellowship with the unfruitful works of darkness, but rather reprove them.(Ephesians 5:11)

> *He that saith unto the wicked, Thou art righteous; him shall the*
> *people curse, nations shall abhor him: But to them that rebuke him shall*
> *be delight, and a good blessing shall come upon them. (Proverbs 24:25)*
>
> *Open rebuke is better than secret love. (Proverbs 27:5)*

The timidity that many Christians often show towards others in standing for what is right is done in such a way so as not to offend anyone to the point of utter ineffectiveness. Evil and sin push forward because of the Christian's fear and desire to be accepted. Edmund Burke said it rightly, that all that is necessary for the triumph of evil is for good men to do nothing. We give the excuse that this is because we love them when in actuality it's a lie. We do it because we love ourselves. It is pride cloaked in false sincerity.

I mentioned earlier about there being all this talk within the church about relevance to unbelievers. This "relevance" always comes at the cost of righteousness. Always. In order to be relevant to an unrighteous world, you must be worldy and worldliness thrives in unrighteousness.

The word of God is eternally relevant to any culture at any time in any place. It's relevant to a person's depravity. It's relevant to their unrighteousness. It's relevant to their need for the Savior. It's relevant to how to obtain eternal life. Its message doesn't need to change nor its presentation. When used in this way, the term "relevant" is a misnomer because the church is not really trying to be relevant. It's trying to be accepted.

The Christian or the church has no business trying to fit in with what the world is doing. The Word is clear that we won't be accepted. They didn't accept our Lord but hated Him (John 15:19-21). So what makes us think that somehow we're going to be accepted by an evil, dark, unholy world because we're a little bit further in history or we have a better gimmick? Not if we're pursuing true righteousness. That's living in some kind of dream world and God's not in it if that's the case.

The church has the responsibility to be the light of the world (Matthew 5:14-16). We can only be this light and express this righteousness when we live in obedience to His word.

For as by one man's disobedience many were made sinners, so by the obedience of one shall many be made righteous. (Romans 5:19)

This point is missed in the church because there's too much focus on whether or not the next program is going to be successful and draw the most congregants to the church, which is backwards. We don't want to draw people to the church. We want to draw people to Jesus Christ through the power of the Holy Spirit. Wolfgang Simson, author of *The House Church Book*, got it right when he said, "Programs are what the church resorts to when the Holy Spirit leaves."[2]

If standing for righteousness is not costing you anything, it's probably not as righteous as you thought. David declared that he would not offer anything to the Lord that cost him nothing (2 Samuel 24:24). The Lord Himself said that no man builds a tower without first counting the cost (Luke 14:28). Standing for true righteousness will cost us something. The litmus test of true righteousness is if it lines up with the principles and tenets of the Holy Scriptures. The more it does, the more it will cost us. This may be the ridicule of peers, loss of friendships/relationships, or finding ourselves ostracized. In the worst cases, it means physical abuse, torture, and death. This is how the world reacts to true righteousness through the church.

Compassion

Out of all the attributes of the church, this is the one that most people identify with and are most familiar, failing to understand that you can't have one without the other. You can't be truly compassionate towards someone until you recognize that it's sin that has them in a grip only Jesus Christ can free them from.

With all of the focus on this, it's surprising to see that the word compassion is used only 41 times in the entire Bible. That's less than one time in each book. There are five words used in the Hebrew and nine in the Greek. Their meanings overlap to a certain extent but they do have subtle differences. We're going to look at the most common from both languages to get a sense of true biblical compassion.

There are two main Hebrew words used in the Old Testament. The first is *chamal* which means to spare, pity, grieve over, or be sorry for. It first appears in Exodus 2:6 when the Pharaoh's daughter had compassion on the baby Moses when she saw him in the Nile river floating in a basket.

The second use is the word *racham* which expresses compassion in the sense of a mother or father for a helpless child. The first occurrence is Deuteronomy 13:17. God commands the children of Israel that when they overcome a city that they should not take of the cursed thing from them so that the Lord would have compassion on them.

Don H. Stewart, Professor of New Testament and Greek at the New Orleans Baptist Seminary, says of this particular translation:

> In scripture, this compassion is protective, reflecting
> the feelings of the more powerful for the inferior.
> The majority of the Bible uses of *racham* has God as
> the subject (the giver) and someone or something in
> the temporal world as the object (recipient).[3]

In the New Testament, the main word used for compassion is the Greek *splanchnizomai*. It means to yearn from the bowels and have pity. The Lord used the term to express the attitude that should be within every believer. It is the word used in the parable of the unforgiving servant (Matthew 18:27), the prodigal son (Luke 15:20), and the good Samaritan (Luke 10:33).

With this understanding, it becomes clear that the church should be filled to the rim with compassion. We know what it's like to walk in darkness and sinfulness, to be lost thinking we have it together yet hastening towards our destruction. We all have experienced the effects and pangs of sin in us, ruling our lives. We know what it's like to be hell-bound.

Knowing this, we should then be compassionate towards others about their sin-sick condition. This is why we pray for them and preach the gospel. Not because it's strictly our Christian duty to do so or because we think we're better than them. It should be because the love of God has been shed abroad in our hearts and we have a genuine biblical compassion for them.

Something is terribly wrong when the only reason why we want to see someone come to faith is so we can rack up some numbers on our belts or fill up a pew. This is prideful, arrogant, selfish, and only fosters false piety. This is not a numbers game. It's a conversion game, so to speak, and we're told by the Lord that there's not going to be a lot of people who find the true road to that end result (Matthew 7:13-14).

True, biblical compassion looks at the condition of an unbeliever and makes the heart of a believer grieve. We're not just speaking of physical needs here in this world though that is a part of it. But more so than anything, it motivates us to be active in the salvation of people's souls. It's often confused with gentleness which speaks more to the way we express that compassion, not having compassion itself.

True compassion confronts a person and is willing to hurt a person's feelings to save their soul. False compassion says and does nothing, walking around on eggshells trying to appease everyone and offend no one. That's not compassion. That's com-promise. In order for compassion to be seen and expressed, we must deny ourselves. Whether it be to give them the gospel or something to eat, true compassion moves to loving action, not just sorrowful feelings. We see this when the Lord Jesus dealt with the multitudes.

And Jesus went forth, and saw a great multitude, and was moved with compassion toward them, and he healed their sick. (Matthew 14:14)

Then Jesus called his disciples unto him, and said, I have compassion on the multitude, because they continue with me now three days, and have nothing to eat: and I will not send them away fasting, lest they faint in the way. (Matthew 15:32)

Mercy

Mercy is a cornerstone of the Christian church. In the most general sense, it's being mindful and sensitive towards the needs and conditions of others, especially those in distress. It's showing them goodness when they are wholly unworthy. It is a universal virtue that should be extended to friend and foe alike, though the Bible seems to place a premium on God showing mercy to those in the household of faith. This sentiment is expressed in the Old Testament where God had mercy on His people more than those outside of the covenant community (Exodus 15:13, Numbers 7:2, 1 Kings 8:23, Psalm 25:10). The law itself spoke of this attitude being expressed between Israelites.

Mercy is distinct from grace. It's been explained this way: mercy is not getting something bad that you do deserve while grace is getting something good that you don't deserve. In other words, mercy is voluntary, not obligatory. We choose whether we are going to have mercy towards someone just as God decided to have mercy towards those He chose.

And he said, I will make all my goodness pass before thee, and I will proclaim the name of the LORD before thee; and will be gracious to whom I will be gracious, and will shew mercy on whom I will shew mercy. (Exodus 33:19)

The Lord Jesus proclaimed a special blessing for those who show mercy.

Blessed are the merciful: for they shall obtain mercy. (Matthew 5:7)

Mercy is a moral aspect of God that Christians like to talk a lot about because without it we wouldn't be saved. However, what's commonly misunderstood is the reality that He balances this perfectly with wrath and judgment. This is where people have a problem, especially when talking about hell. They like a loving, compassionate, and merciful God. That they can live with. It's the wrathful God of judgment that they have a problem with because it's that God who magnifies the sinfulness of their condition. Dan Parker, associate professor of pastoral ministry at Leavell College explains:

> God's justice and righteousness cannot be overlooked in this matter of mercy. Exodus 34:7 makes it clear that God's judgment will override His mercy where man's sinful rebellion turns away from His righteousness and love. Here God's mercy is manifested in His slow action and deferred punishment, not in ignoring sin and refusing to act in wrath....God's wrath is the resulting action against man's rebellion after His mercy has been exhausted.[4]

This is seen in 2 Samuel 7:15 when God declares that He took His mercy from Saul because of Saul's continued disobedience and eventual apostasy. It is also explained in graphic terms in Romans 1 where God takes away His mercy because man refuses to glorify Him as God in the way He has revealed Himself (Romans 1:18-32). Many times this includes the knowledge of who He is which leads them to believe in false Gods and false ideas about God. This is why there are so many false religions in the world.

To think that God is just going to be eternally indifferent to a person's sin is presumptuous and is tempting God which the Bible warns against doing. God is merciful but His mercy has a limit and only endures forever to those that love Him.

And shewing mercy unto thousands of them that love me, and keep my commandments. (Exodus 20:6)

As I mentioned before, this list is not exhaustive. However, I believe that these are the pillars of the church that when rightly exhibited in proper balance, will produce the other attributes in due course. I simply bring attention to these four because in the current spiritual climate, they are far too often overlooked or altogether ignored.

References

1. Holman Bible Dictionary, D. Jefferey Mooney, pg. 1400

2. The House Church Book, Wolfgang Simson, pg.

3. Holman Bible Dictionary, Don H. Stewart, pg. 325

4. Holman Bible Dictionary, Dan Parker, pg. 1106

Chapter 4

The Purpose of the Church to the World

"This evangelistic work of declaring the gospel is the primary ministry that the church has to the world." - Wayne Grudem

THERE IS ONE trait underneath the umbrella of glorifying God which is a distinct duty for His church alone to the world. This is to spread the gospel.

Spread the Gospel

As the people of God, we are entrusted with a mission. That mission is reconciling the world to God.

And all things are of God, who hath reconciled us to himself by Jesus Christ, and hath given to us the ministry of reconciliation. (2 Corinthians 5:18).

This is done through the faithful and effective preaching of the gospel. To some this may seem like a foregone conclusion. Simply mentioning it should be the end of the matter. Everyone in the church knows this, right?

Well, though the basic concept that the church should spread the gospel is widely published, proclaimed, and even understood, the question that needs to be asked, especially today, is what is the gospel? Is it the health, wealth, and prosperity message? Is it righteousness by works? Is it finding Jesus (as if He was lost) and having Him come in, heal you, and make your life better? What exactly is the true gospel?

The confusion of defining the gospel is exacerbated by the reality of the Christian faith being under attack incessantly by an increasingly hostile world that questions the veracity of the scriptures. This has found its way into so-called Christian churches. This is crucial because if we don't get the terms of the gospel right from the beginning, then we run the risk of making false converts instead of true and faithful witnesses of the faith. So it's essential that the church gets this right.

The word "gospel" is translated from two Greek words which are derivatives from one another. *Euaggelion* is a derivative of *euag-*

gelizo. They mean "a good message" or to "announce good news." They are a compound of the words *eu* (good) and *aggelos* (a messenger).

We can conclude from this that the message the church brings to the world is good. However, the world's definition of what's good and God's definition are two different things. Rest assured that God's definition of what is good is legitimate. Let's look at the scriptures and see what they have to say about this "good message".

Man's Dilemma

If you go into some sanctuaries today and gather with the church, you may hear an altar call or an invitation to Christ at the conclusion. Here the gospel is supposedly preached and those who want to make a commitment to Christ are invited to come to the front to dedicate themselves to following the Lord. More and more, what is omitted from that whole message is explaining man's dilemma in relation to God.

There are actually two facets of a full gospel message: the bad and the good. It's the bad news of the gospel which absolutely has to precede the good news in order for the good news to be magnified to its proper place. This may seem like an oxymoron but it isn't. People need to understand why the good news is so good. If we simply give them a feel good speech that strokes their egos and assuages their emotions, we're not giving them the full gospel and we are deceiving them into believing a lie instead of the truth.

For example, let's say someone comes to you and says, "Jesus loves you and He has a plan and purpose for your life." Now there are a couple different ways you could respond to that. You might say that you couldn't care less what Jesus thinks, that it's your life and you'll live it how you want to live it. You might nod in agreement and think that's a nice sentiment for Jesus to have about you. You might say that you already know that and that you're living in the purpose that He wants for you. Or you might simply ignore them and continue on your merry way.

In any of these hypothetical situations, there is absolutely no urgency for you to continue on with the exchange. It is simply information with no efficacy that demands a response of inquiry. It sounds good and it might pique your curiosity a bit but that's about the extent of it.

However, it would be a different story if someone were to come up to you and say, "I don't know if you know this but your soul and very existence are in danger." Now we're looking at a little different response ("Why would they say that?" "Why would I be in danger?" "How dare they make that claim! I'm going to give them a little piece of my mind!"). The efficacy of the statement produces urgency and inquiry. Even if the response is hostile, it still has evoked a response that has gotten the attention of the hearer and engages them much more than the previous one.

You can almost guarantee that they will remember that statement.

We can break down the "bad news" of the gospel into four parts: Man is evil. God is good. God allows no evil in heaven. All evil goes to hell.

Man Is Evil

The general idea in humanism is that man is basically good. There are exceptions to this but all in all, most people believe they are inherently good. Even some Christians have given in to this false notion.

The truth is that in the eyes of God, man is *far* from good. The exact opposite to be precise. Man is evil.

The LORD looked down from heaven upon the children of men, to see if there were any that did understand, and seek God. They are all gone aside, they are all together become filthy: there is none that doeth good, no, not one. (Psalms 14:2-3)

Not only is man not good, he's unclean. The word filthy is translated from the Hebrew *alach* meaning morally corrupt.

I feel I should pause here and explain something before I move further. When I say man when speaking about his dilemma, I'm speaking in reference to mankind. I'm speaking of everyone who is a human being. Since woman was created from man (Genesis 2:22-23), it is wholly appropriate to say man in the general sense. Some of you may be puzzled at that but feminism being what it is today, it really does need to be clarified to avoid any confusion that I'm leaving out women and children. On the contrary, it means every human being on the face of the planet.

That being said, no one is exempt from that proclamation. If you are a human being, you do not seek God, do not do good, and you are morally corrupt according to the scriptures.

Not only is man corrupt in his actions, he is infected at his very core.

The heart is deceitful above all things, and desperately wicked: who can know it? (Jeremiah 7:9)

Here the scriptures declare that the very heart of man is the most deceitful thing in existence along with being wicked. The Hebrew for desperately wicked is *anash* which means feeble, frail, incurable.

Two phrases that are bandied about today are, "Just follow your heart." or "Look into your heart." The first is a recipe for disaster given the condition of our hearts. The second is a nightmare that no one can come away feeling good about if they are being honest and transparent with themselves. The majority of the world is totally oblivious to just how wicked their hearts are. By extension, if their heart is desperately wicked, the person is.

Children are a simple illustration of this. We say that children learn bad behavior and that is true to an extent. However, they learn it more severely, not entirely. Let's not confuse innocence with goodness. These are two totally different things.

Children innately know how to do wrong if you leave them alone long enough. Ever see a two year old go on a rampage? Not pretty. You find yourself saying multiple times, "Don't touch that!" "Stop it!" "No!" "You're going to get a whoopin!" (To the chagrin of the politically correct, some of us do spank our children). Having to tell them once because they were ignorant is one thing. Having to tell them five times in ten minutes is disobedient and evil. Their parents didn't tell them to disobey. Quite the contrary. They tell them to obey but children will disobey, just like we disobey God because at our core, we're desperately wicked.

The Lord Jesus had the most pungent words to say about man when addressing His listeners in the Sermon on the Mount.

*If ye then, **being evil** (emphasis mine), know how to give good gifts unto your children, how much more shall your Father which is in heaven give good things to them that ask him? (Matthew 7:11)*

Most people that would hear that would think it's the boldest, rawest, most arrogant statement He could make. This is because when a person thinks about themselves, they normally lean towards looking at themselves as slightly bad or naughty. But evil is reserved for folks like Hitler, Stalin, and Osama Bin Laden. For them to look at themselves as evil is an affront to their sensibilities. What they fail to realize is that their sensibilities are determined by that same corrupt heart that makes them so offended. The first one the heart deceives is its owner and it tells them that they are not that bad. That they are good.

The observant reader may ask the question, "If man is so evil, how come some of the most compassionate and good things are done by unbelievers like Ghandi?" This is a fair question.

In the book of Isaiah, the prophet declares:

But we are all as an unclean thing, and all our righteousnesses are as filthy rags; and we all do fade as a leaf; and our iniquities, like the wind, have taken us away (Isaiah 64:6).

The actions that are committed by an unbeliever are not committed in faith towards God with a love for Him. Anything not done in this capacity is as filthy rags to God. To get the clear picture, the word "filthy" is translated *ed* which refers to a bloody rag during the menstrual cycle of a woman.

An act can be right from the perspective that it benefits another positively. But ultimately it is not good. It is tainted by the sin of the individual committing it because it is not done in faith towards God. Nothing a person does "in the flesh", outside of faith, can please God.

So then they that are in the flesh cannot please God (Romans 8:8).

And the writer of Hebrews echoes this:

But without faith it is impossible to please him: (Hebrews 11:6).

Man is dead in sins. We who are saved know this because it was the position we were in before we came to Christ:

And you, being dead in your sins and the uncircumcision of your flesh, hath he quickened together with him, having forgiven you all trespasses; (Colossians 2:13)

And you hath he quickened, who were dead in trespasses and sins; Wherein in time past ye walked according to the course of this world, according to the prince of the power of the air, the spirit that now worketh in the children of disobedience: Among whom also we all had our conversation in times past in the lusts of our flesh, fulfilling the desires of the flesh and of the mind; and were by nature the children of wrath, even as others. (Ephesians 2:1-3)

Man is in a state of rebellion. He has no interest in the things of God and has no privileges in relation to Him. God is his enemy and He is not pleased with them and makes this known clearly:

*God judgeth the righteous, and **God is angry with the wicked every day** (emphasis mine).* (Psalm 7:11)

The great reformer, Martin Luther, said this about sinners and God's attitude towards them:

> God is not hostile towards sinners, only towards
> unbelievers.[1]

At the end of the day, no matter how one feels about themselves in terms of what they do, outside of Christ, man is unregenerate, unholy, depraved, desperately wicked, and evil. That includes Ghandi.

God (and Only God) Is Good

In comparison, God is good. As a matter of fact, the Bible is clear that God alone is good. In other words, God in His very essence is good. He is the epitome and personification of it. Without Him, there is no good.

Good and upright is the LORD: therefore will he teach sinners in the way. (Psalm 25:8)

The LORD is good, a stronghold in the day of trouble; and he knoweth them that trust in him. (Nahum 1:7)

And he said unto him, Why callest thou me good? There is none good but one, that is, God (Matthew 19:17a).

Today, we use phrases like, "They're good people" or "I'm a good person" or "I do good deeds." However, as was stated before, on our best day, all of our "good" deeds are nothing but filthy rags and vanity.

Behold, thou hast made my days as an handbreadth; and mine age is as nothing before thee: verily every man at his best state is altogether vanity. (Psalms 39:5)

The reason for this has been explained but I'll elaborate even further here; that man at his core is evil, wicked, and depraved so everything that he touches is corrupted. It's a poisonous apple from the tainted tree. The act of producing apples may be right but the apples, because the tree is tainted, are not good.

Evil Will Not Exist In Heaven Eternally

The news shocked all in the palace, piercing to the hearts and souls of everyone. They discovered him in his bed. The king was dead, having died of natural causes in his sleep.

"Where has he gone?" one of the king's advisers inquired.

"He's in heaven now," replied others gathered around.

"No," said one of his closest aides. "I served this king for many years and traveled with him extensively. He loved to travel and would talk about his trips incessantly beforehand. Every detail was planned and anticipated. But I never heard him say a word about traveling to heaven. It was a journey for which I saw no preparation. No. I am quite sure he has not gone to heaven."

The scene above is one that many people have gone through at funerals around the world. The reactions are the same. They presume that the deceased has gone to heaven because they have believed the lie that humans are basically good. But sentimental feelings and emotional outbreaks don't change the spiritual reality.

J.C Ryle in his book *Holiness*, points out:

Heaven is a holy place. The Lord of heaven is a holy Being. The angels are holy creatures. Holiness is written on everything in heaven...How shall we ever be at home and happy in heaven if we die unholy? Death works no change. The grave makes no alteration. Each will rise again with the same character in which He breathed his last.[2]

Understanding that mankind is evil and that a right act does not make a good person, unregenerate man has no hope of ever making it to Heaven.

God's holiness is so profound and so striking that when in His presence, men are humbled, awed, and terrified.

I have heard of thee by the hearing of the ear: but now mine eye seeth thee. Wherefore I abhor myself, and repent in dust and ashes. (Job 42:5,6)

And when I saw him, I fell at his feet as dead. And he laid his right hand upon me, saying unto me, Fear not; I am the first and the last (Revelations 1:17).

Sinful humans cannot stand in the presence of God because God will not look on evil and do nothing.

Thou art of purer eyes than to behold evil, and canst not look on iniquity (Habakkuk 1:13a)

As smoke is driven away, so drive them away: as wax melteth before the fire, so let the wicked perish at the presence of God. (Psalms 68:2).

That no flesh should glory in his presence (1 Corinthians 1:29).

In the Old Testament, God's presence was said to reside in the tabernacle in the Most Holy of Holies above the Ark of the Covenant. Only the high priest was allowed to go in and that only once a year. To do it at any other time or in any manner besides the prescribed one meant instant death. Tradition records that a rope was tied to the ankle of the high priest in case something happened that was awry and he was struck dead.

Being in the presence of God is no joke. An unholy, unregenerate, depraved, evil man cannot stand in His presence and live forever. Therefore they will not be in heaven. And, quite frankly, if that is their condition, that's simply not where they would want to be.

And this is the condemnation, that light is come into the world, and men loved darkness rather than light, because their deeds were evil (John 3:19).

And there shall in no wise enter into it any thing that defileth, neither whatsoever worketh abomination, or maketh a lie: but they which are written in the Lamb's book of life (Revelations 21:27).

All Evil Goes to Hell

Today, hell is a place not many people want to talk about, especially among the church on Sunday. What is becoming more common is sappy, unbiblical heresies, lies, or omissions so as not to offend the congregation. It is a rare occasion when you get pastors and preachers admonishing from the pulpits like Charles Spurgeon, who said:

> As the Lord liveth, sinner, thou standest on a single
> plank over the mouth of hell and that plank is rotten.
> Thou hangest over the pit by a solitary rope, and the
> strands of that rope are breaking.[3]

In an article in the March 1991 issue of U.S. News and World

Report entitled *Hell's Sober Comeback,* the question was asked whether the respondents thought they were going to heaven or hell. Seventy-eight percent thought they were going to heaven. Four percent thought they were going to hell. Quite frankly, the reality is more like the other way around.

Enter ye in at the strait gate: for wide is the gate, and broad is the way, that leadeth to destruction, and many there be which go in thereat: Because strait is the gate, and narrow is the way, which leadeth unto life, ***and few there be that find it*** *(emphasis mine). (Matthew 7:13-14)*

Hell is not a fictional place that parents make up to scare their children into behaving. Hell is a real, literal place which the Lord Jesus talked about extensively while He was here on earth. As a matter of fact, the Lord talked more about hell than He talked about God's love (which He never talked about when calling people to repentance). If we're supposed to be imitators of God (Ephesians 5:1) and Jesus is God (John 1:1), then why are we not preaching about the dangers of hell to those who are on their way there since that's what He did?

Hell is a place of torment and darkness where there will be weeping and gnashing of teeth (Matthew 13:41-42, Luke 13:28, 16:19-31). It is a place that the unrighteous, ungodly, and impenitent sinner goes after death and will be thrown into the lake of fire where those who reside there will burn and suffer for eternity (Revelations 20:10,14-15).

As you might expect, people don't want to go there.

So man, who is able to make a volitional decision about right and wrong in his current condition because of God's mercy which is extended to everyone on the planet, is on his way to hell. Everyone. No exceptions. He knows right and wrong and chooses wrong. Why? It has nothing to do with right acts. It has to do with sinful, corrupt hearts. Our very nature is tainted and defiled.

This is where the gospel begins: informing an unregenerate sinner that they are in danger of hell, not that they have a disease and that Jesus is the cure. Soft sells like that seek to lessen the reality of what the Bible says, taking the blame away from where it needs to be which is on the individual. God puts it there. So should we. Whether a listener gets offended or not is really not our concern. Our concern should be for their soul, not their ego. Their reaction is inconsequential. The truth isn't. It is an act of love to tell them about their dilemma first because the situation is of utmost importance. People must come to understand and realize how serious and heinous sin is to a Most Holy God.

God's Heart

As the clarion call goes out to all people that they are in a precarious spiritual situation of eternal consequences, we can now begin to tell them about the heart of God. This is important because of how God has been vilified, maligned, and misrepresented not only by those who oppose Him but by those falsely representing Him. The world must understand the real God of the Bible, not the one that people react to because they have a personal problem with Him or the one they create from their own minds.

There are three main points that people need to understand about God in reference to salvation: God loves them, God has a purpose for them, and does not will for them to perish.

God Loves You

Love. It's one of the most highly charged words in the English language. It's used all of the time to describe how we feel and what we desire. It's often used so much that it tends to lose its effect on the human soul because of the carelessness by which we employ it. We become desensitized to the depths of what it means.

When many people think of love, they think of a feeling. An emotional state. Yet the deepest love is not simply felt. It lives, breathes, moves and has Being. It is a Person, for God is love (1 John 4:8).

God is eternally giving of Himself to a creation that spurns and hates Him, of reaching out to them while they flee His presence at every turn. God is always the initiator because the Bible says:

Herein is love, not that we loved God, but that he loved us, and sent his Son to be the propitiation for our sins (1 John 4:10).

The state of man, left to his own devices. He would never seek God. Therefore, God made the first move.

But God commendeth his love toward us, in that, while we were yet sinners, Christ died for us (Romans 5:8).

God's love transcends human love. Human love is most often conditional, has limits, and reaches only a short distance. God's love is unconditional, is limitless, and knows no bounds. Even the human love that we have is because God gives us the ability to love. Even when we find glimpses of love that is not common, we understand that it's not common. We understand that love that is truly unconditional, showing mercy and grace to enemies and going beyond the depths to give of itself is a love that can only be supernatural. We recognize, when we are true to ourselves, that we do not have the capacity to love like that in and of ourselves.

During the time of Jesus, the Greeks used three words to express love: *eros, phileo,* and a*gapao/agape.*

Eros love is where we get the word erotic. It is a sexual, fleshly love.

Phileo is tender affection that one may have towards a friend or loved one. This is a very common use of the word love in the New Testament.

Agapao/agape is used often and God is always the source. Not once is it man. This is the love that God calls His followers to have towards Him as to imitate Him. It is this love that God has towards the unbelieving, unregenerate, evil, unholy, wicked sinner. This can only be done by having His love through obeying His word.

If ye keep my commandments, ye shall abide in my love; even as I have kept my Father's commandments, and abide in his love. (John 15:10)

In the song *His Love...Reaching*, it paints the picture of this perfectly:

> Right from the beginning God's love has reached, and from the beginning man has refused to understand. But love went on reaching, offering itself. Love offered the eternal, we wanted the immediate. Love offered deep joy, we wanted thrills. Love offered freedom, we wanted license. Love offered communion with God Himself, we wanted to worship at the shrines of our own minds. Love offered peace, we wanted approvals for our wars. Even yet, love went on reaching. And still today after two thousand years, patiently, lovingly Christ is reaching out to us today. Right through the chaos of our world, through the confusion of our minds. He is reaching, longing to share with us the very being of God. His love is still longing, His love is still reaching,

right past the shackles of my mind.[4]

God loves you and me. God loves everyone because He can do nothing else. God is love.

Though this truth cannot be expressed to its full weight, if that was the end of the story and we stop there, we're still all going to hell. "You mean to tell me that I'm still on my way to hell?" If we stop there, yes because God's love is born out of His holiness and as we said before, evil and sin cannot stand in the presence of God and have nothing done about it.

But we're not stopping there because that's not the end of the story.

God Has a Purpose for You

God does not go through the trouble of creating man without giving him a purpose.

For I know the thoughts that I think toward you, saith the LORD, thoughts of peace, and not of evil, to give you an expected end. (Jeremiah 29:11).

Though in context this is God speaking to Israel, I argue He has these same thoughts to everyone, especially when it comes to salvation (see next section). People have come to an erroneous notion that God is sitting up on His throne in heaven just waiting for someone to do wrong so He can make their lives miserable and afterward send them to hell. He just doesn't want anyone to have any fun.

I'm here to tell you that it just ain't so.

In the Westminster Shorter Catechism, it describes the chief end of man which is to glorify God and to enjoy Him forever. That means that we cannot fulfill God's ultimate purpose for our existence without serving Him.

The question might be asked that if God is sovereign, won't He use whoever He wants whenever He wants? Yes, He will. But what I'm discussing here is not earthly destiny but existential purpose. We cannot fulfill that purpose if we are in rebellion against Him. You can rest assured that no one in hell is willfully glorifying God.

God Desires for Man to Be Saved

God is very clear about what He desires for rebellious mankind:

Say unto them, As I live, saith the Lord GOD, I have no pleasure in the death of the wicked; but that the wicked turn from his way and live: turn ye, turn ye from your evil ways; for why will ye die, O house of Israel? (Ezekiel 33:11)

The Lord delights in mercy (Matthew 9:13). As a matter of fact, the phrase, "His mercy endureth forever" is repeated 35 times in the book of Psalms alone. The Bible states in 1 Peter 3:9 that God is not willing that any should perish in hell but that everyone would repent and turn to life. The fact that He pleads with man, an act that He certainly is not obligated to do, shows His heart in and of itself. The false picture that has been painted of God is due to bad teaching along with biblical ineptness and ultimately depraved hearts.

God has done everything on His end to provide a way out. He has provided forgiveness for the evil that we perpetrate against Him, first and foremost, and against each other. It is what people need and really want from the depths of their soul if they would dare to face the pit that is inside of their innermost being.

Secular humanist and novelist Marghanita Laski was reported to have said in 1988 before she died:

> What I envy the most about you Christians is your
>
> forgiveness; I have nobody to forgive me.[5]

Forgiveness is here and it is free to receive. God loves to set people free.

For this is good and acceptable in the sight of God our Saviour; Who will have all men to be saved, and to come unto the knowledge of the truth. (1 Timothy 2:3-4)

God's Solution

Knowing God's heart will not solve the problem. Again, if that was the end of the story, everyone would still go to hell. Something has to be done about sin.

The Penalty for Sin is Death

The Bible lays out that there is only one price for sin. That is death.

For the wages of sin is death, (Romans 6:23a)

As righteousness tendeth to life: so he that pursueth evil pursueth it to his own death. (Proverbs 11:19)

Behold, all souls are mine; as the soul of the father, so also the soul of the son is mine: the soul that sinneth, it shall die. (Ezekiel 18:4)

There is no such thing as small sins. The price is for one sin. Ever. In life. Not only as a committed act externally, but as an evil desire internally.

We may look at this and think that this is just overkill. However, we fail to understand the total destructiveness of sin and how atrocious and offensive it is to God. We make light of it and give excuses for it. God doesn't, which is why there is a hell. This is why the Lord can say:

For my thoughts are not your thoughts, neither are your ways my ways, saith the LORD. For as the heavens are higher than the earth, so are my ways higher than your ways, and my thoughts than your thoughts. (Isaiah 55:8-9)

We simply don't get it.

Theologian Dr. Francis Schaeffer in his book *The God Who Is There*, describes how sin has infected everything known to man:

When man fell, various divisions took place. The

first and basic division is between man, who has
revolted, and God. All other divisions flow from
that....For, secondly, man was separated from himself. This gives rise to the psychological problems
in life. Thirdly, man was separated from other
men, leading to the sociological problems of life.

Fourthly, man was separated from nature.[6]

In short, sin has polluted and destroyed everything. The enor-
mity of this reality is staggering and only God truly grasps the full
ramifications, though He gives us glimpses through His word
and history itself. This is the reason why there were so many sacrifices in the Old Testament . Something had to die to take the pun-
ishment that God requires.

*And almost all things are by the law purged with blood; and without
shedding of blood is no remission. (Hebrews 9:22)*

However, this was merely a covering for sin. The blood of
bulls and goats did not take away the sin problem. They were tem-
porary and symbolic.

*For it is not possible that the blood of bulls and of goats should take
away sins. (Hebrews 10:4)*

These sacrifices had to be ongoing and they also were an
example of how sin would eventually be dealt with once and for
all.

Jesus Died in Our Place

In order to eradicate sin once and for all, something else had to be done. Enter Jesus the Christ.

Jesus is called the "Lamb of God".

The next day John seeth Jesus coming unto him, and saith, Behold the Lamb of God, which taketh away the sin of the world. (John 1:29)

This was a reference to the Old Testament and would have been very familiar to the Jews since it was the animal used for the feast of Passover (Exodus 12). As the blood of the lamb was smeared on the doorposts of the houses in Egypt so that the angel of death would "pass over" the children of Israel, the same is used of Jesus the Christ. Those who accept His sacrifice as *the* sacrifice for their sins, shed on the cross for all of mankind, will be passed over for eternal damnation in hell. Later, when the Levitical law was given, this lamb sacrifice was supposed to be continual, every evening and morning. In addition, it was to be a lamb without defect. Perfect and flawless. This is the Lord Jesus.

For we have not an High Priest which cannot be touched with the feeling of our infirmities; but was in all points tempted like as we are yet without sin. (Hebrews 4:15)

This is the reason why no other human being was sufficient. They are tainted with sin. Jesus the Christ is not. Therefore, His sacrifice is sufficient not only to take away sin but destroy its power over us.

Isaiah prophesied about this in 53:7 and Paul reiterates this in 1 Corinthians 5:7:

He was oppressed, and he was afflicted, yet he opened not his mouth: he is brought as a lamb to the slaughter, and as a sheep before her shearers is dumb, so he openeth not his mouth.

Purge out therefore the old leaven, that ye may be a new lump, as ye are unleavened. For even Christ our passover is sacrificed for us:

Even in heaven now, Christ is referred to as the Lamb that was slain (Revelation 5:12-13).

God did not just have sorrow over man's condition but has done something about it.

Faith In the Sacrifice of Jesus Saves Us

Faith in the Lord Jesus, that His sacrifice is enough to do away with our sins once and for all., That He is God in the flesh, is what's needed to be saved.

That if thou shalt confess with thy mouth the Lord Jesus, and shalt believe in thine heart that God hath raised him from the dead, thou shalt be saved. (Romans 10:9)

To believe means far more than what we think it means. It is translated from the Greek word *pisteuo* which Dr. MacArthur explains:

> To trust, rely on, or have faith in. When used of sal-
> vation, this word usually occurs in the present tense

("is believing") which stresses that faith is not simply

a one time event, but an ongoing condition.[7]

Did you get that? Re-read that again so you don't miss it.

To believe in anyone else or in any other way is not true saving faith. Jesus Himself declared:

I am the way, the truth, and the light. No man cometh unto the Father but by me. (John 14:6)

Verily, verily, I say unto you, He that entereth not by the door into the sheepfold, but climbeth up some other way, the same is a thief and a robber. (John 10:1)

Neither is there salvation in any other: for there is none other name under heaven given among men, whereby we must be saved. (Acts 4:12)

I said therefore unto you, that ye shall die in your sins: for if ye believe not that I am he, ye shall die in your sins. (John 8:24)

It is only through faith in Christ, God in the flesh, that His sacrifice was sufficient to deal with the evil and sin within us. He is Lord, God over all and being so, has saved us from hell and translated us into His glorious kingdom eternally.

Dr. MacArthur explains the three aspects involved in true saving faith:

> Mental - the mind understands the gospel and the
> truth about Christ (Romans 10:14-17).
>
> Emotional - one embraces the truth of those facts

with sorrow over sin and joy over God's mercy and

grace (Romans 6:17, 15:13).

Volitional - the sinner submits his will to Christ and

trusts in Him alone as the only hope of salvation.[8]

This leads us to the last detail of the true gospel.

We Repent from Our Ways and Turn to God's Ways

Understanding all of this, we repent. It is becoming more common for this part of the gospel to be left out in churches today or in just a simple presentation of the gospel in a one on one situation.

"Repent" is translated from the Greek word *metanoeo* which literally means "to think differently of or reconsider." When it comes to true salvation, this means turning from our ways and turning to God's ways as laid out in the Bible. Simply giving mental assent to the reality of the Lord's sacrifice on the cross or that He is the Son of God is not enough for true saving faith. This goes hand in hand with the volitional portion just presented.

Revivalist and historian J. Edwin Orr gives a great example in reference to this:

Does "repent and believe the gospel" imply that the sinner must do two things to be saved, and not the one only? The exhortation is really only one requirement.

> The instruction, "Leave London and go to Los Angeles,"
> sounds like a two-fold request but really is only one;
> it is impossible to go to Los Angeles without leaving
> London.[9]

In other words, without repentance, there is no true saving faith. There is no salvation.

The mark of true repentance is the fruit of the Spirit (Galatians 5:22-23). It's having an inner desire to want to please God in every area of our lives. It's a consuming passion to represent God in truth as ambassadors of His kingdom. We do this by keeping His commandments by the power of the Spirit as an expression of love towards the Lord (John 14:15), all the while growing in our knowledge of Him (2 Peter 1:3).

This is the true gospel.

The Mission

Armed with the true gospel that the Lord has left with us, it is incumbent upon His people to take that message to the world.

When Jesus resurrected from the dead, He gave an explicit command. We find this in Matthew 28:19-20:

Go ye therefore, and make disciples of all the nations, baptizing them into the name of the Father and of the Son and of the Holy Spirit: teaching them to observe all things whatsoever I commanded you: and lo, I am with you always, even unto the end of the world.

Within these two verses we have the basic call and method of evangelism.

Four Commands of Evangelism

Command 1 - Go

Believe it or not, more and more churches are dropping the ball at this first step. Many times it's the exact opposite. We don't go. We stay and tell others to come.

The word "go" here is the Greek *poreuomai* which means travel, depart, or continue on one's journey. Dr. Warren Wiersbe explains:

> The Greek verb translated go is...a present participle (going)....Jesus said, "While you are going, make disciples of all nations." No matter where we are, we should be witnesses for Jesus Christ and seek to win others to Him.[10]

Of course, we have missions and that's good and is part of evangelism. No question. But when Jesus went out and about, He went to His immediate neighborhood. He went to where the people were at and the people followed. His Sermon on the Mount is just that, on a mount outside. He met in people's houses like Zacchaeus (Luke 19:2-10) and Jairus (Mark 5:22, 35-43). He went to the temple because that was the hangout spot back then. He declares:

And Jesus saith unto him, The foxes have holes, and the birds of the air have nests; but the Son of man hath not where to lay his head. (Matthew 8:20)

His ministry was itinerant and He called His followers to have the same kind of ministry dynamic when it came to evangelism. Every Christian is a minister and therefore has the responsibility of spreading the gospel to a lost world.

It's important to note that the Lord wasn't speaking just to those disciples, but to anyone who called themselves His disciple. We don't wait to bring them to someone else so that they can give them the gospel. We, meaning His church, are responsible to bring the nations the gospel. This is why it's so important to get the terms of the gospel correct from the beginning.

Command 2 - Make Disciples

As we're going, we should make disciples of those who repent and confess allegiance to the Lord Jesus. Making a disciple is not the same as making a convert. A convert is made when the gospel is preached and believed. Making a disciple comes after that.

The word "disciple" comes from a Latin root that basically means "a student or pupil." In the Greek, it was normally related to someone who followed a particular school of thought religiously or philosophically. A disciple had to be committed to learn, study, and eventually do the same thing that was being done with them to others.

When we commit to make disciples, it means investing time and care into that individual that God has placed into our lives to edify, support, and help in their growth in the faith. This isn't elementary school where you just drop the kids off so that the teacher can teach them and call it a day. It's a group effort, helping to hold that believer accountable until they can walk on their own and are prepared to do the same thing.

Making a disciple is work. This is probably the reason why the church has shunned it so much. It means taking time to pray for them regularly, inquire about their lives, encourage and teach them. It's being dedicated not only to their spiritual well being, but all facets of their lives.

Command 3 - Teach

Tied directly to making a disciple, we should teach them what it means to be a true disciple of Christ. This is encompassed in regular Bible study, prayer, and fellowship with the saints. It does not mean that every Christian is going to be a gifted teacher and orator. It does mean that disciples should be able to handle the word of God and present it in a way where a believer can apply the teachings to their lives, thus glorifying God in heaven.

No one knows everything except the Lord. Teachers need

teachers. The process is cyclical. It's a perpetual case of disciples making disciples when implemented biblically. It's not a numbers game to get more people added to the church. The trend today is to look at the size of a church congregation as a measure of its spirituality. This cannot be further from the truth. Many so-called mega-churches propagate messages that are neither scriptural or sound doctrinally. Their size is many times nothing but a measure of how many people are being led astray with bad teaching. This is not just mega-churches (and not all mega-churches are like this) but a good portion of churches throughout the world, small, medium, and large. The size of a congregation has nothing to do with whether a church has solid, biblical, sound teaching. How that church rightly handles, preaches, and teaches of the word of God is. The number of congregants is not a measure of a church's success or failure. Just a measure of the number of people that attend their gatherings. That's it.

Sound teaching is foundational to the church and therefore we are encouraged to make sure that we hold onto it. Paul, in his letter to Titus, said:

Holding fast the faithful word as he hath been taught, that he may be able by sound doctrine both to exhort and to convince the gainsayers. (Titus 1:9)

The phrase "sound doctrine" means healthy, uncorrupt instruction or teaching. R. Albert Mohler Jr. explains:

The Christian church cannot avoid teaching and thus must formulate a framework for understanding and teaching the basic rudiments and principles of the faith and developing those basic doctrines into more comprehensive and thorough understandings. Without such a framework, the church has no coherent system of beliefs and no means of discriminating between true and false beliefs...The Bible is the controlling and ultimate authority for all matters of Christian belief and practice. Experience, reason, and tradition are to be judged by Scripture, and Scripture is not to be judged by other authorities. This principle has characterized the church in every period of doctrinal strength and purity. When compromised, false teachings and heresies inevitably follows.[11]

A question that is often raised is, "How do I know if the teaching is sound or unsound?" Simple. Know the Bible for yourself. Study it. As the scripture says:

Study to shew thyself approved unto God, a workman who needeth not to be ashamed, rightly dividing the word of truth. (2 Timothy 2:15)

Much of the spiritual and biblical confusion today is not due only to false or erroneous teaching, but lazy listeners and bad students of the word. Those claiming to be Christians have Bibles sitting unread in homes for weeks at a time. If they do crack it open, it's on Sunday simply because everyone else is doing it. The Word of God does not spark a thirst and a hunger for it because the heart is not desiring it. Too many other things come in and push our attention away from the Word, away from us knowing not only the truth about God but the truth in general. When this happens, people will fall for anything.

The body of Christ can prevent this through exegetical, expositional teaching of the scriptures with a focus on obedience to it. A disciple who doesn't obey is not a disciple at all. Partial obedience is full disobedience.

Command 4 - Baptize

Baptism is considered to be a foundational practice within the church of Christ. It has become so central to the faith that theologians like Martin Luther and John Calvin stated that without it, a congregation is not considered a real church.

Baptism is the public display that a person has died to the life that they lived in sin, buried it, and has resurrected with Christ to a new life in holiness and righteousness just as the Lord did bodily. It is an immersion of that person in water as a symbol of the cleansing of their sins and their identification with Christ. It signals that the individual will now be held accountable to uphold the teachings of the Lord as they walk with Him for the rest of their lives.

The Lord Jesus thought baptism was so important that He was also baptized by John, his cousin (Matthew 3:14-15). When He ascended to heaven, it was what he commanded His disciples to do also.

There's a specificity to the baptism, as it should be in the name of the Father, the Son, and the Holy Spirit. Here we see the exact God we are identifying with, the triune God spoken of in the scriptures. The "name" is not plural but singular, indicating the Oneness of the Godhead of whom we serve.

It's important to note that immersion is the sense in which the word "baptism" is derived (baptizo). Jewish and first century Christians were baptized by full body immersion. It is the only form of baptism (the others being pouring and sprinkling) that effectively presents the death, burial, and resurrection of the believer with Christ. In addition, only those who could bear witness to the reality of what Christ had done for them were considered candidates for baptism.

L. Paige Patterson, President of the Southwestern Baptist Theological Seminary and Professor of Theology, writes:

> Accordingly, the only appropriate candidate for the witness of baptism is someone who has something about which he can bear witness. There is no precedent

for infant baptism in the New Testament; in addition,

only one who has experienced regeneration can give

a genuine witness to that experience.[12]

Baptism is symbolic only and does not guarantee that an individual is a redeemed, regenerated, born again believer. To the contrary, there are many who go through the act only as a religious tradition, not because they have repented and turned to Christ. They're simply wet sinners who have falsely testified to the world about their witness and are on their way to hell just like any other unregenerate sinner. Even so, a person should be baptized when they have confessed faith in Jesus Christ. The details of the heart are up to God.

This is evangelism and discipleship, the Bible way.

Conclusion

We have looked at two of the purposes of the church which is glorify God and spread the gospel. In essence, the purposes can be broken down into three relational elements:

1. The church's relation to God
2. The church's relation to the world
3. The church's relation to itself.

It is the last relational element we'll focus on in the next chapter.

References

1. Martin Luther, A Treatise On Good Works, pg 55

2. J.C. Ryle, Holiness: Its Nature, Hindrances, Difficulties and Roots, pg 53

3. Charles Haddon Spurgeon, Spurgeon's Sermons, Volume 1, pg. 294

4. Gloria Gaither, Hymns From the Family of God, pg. 200

5. Marghanita Laski, 1001 Quotes, Illustrations, and Humorous Stories for Preachers, Teachers, and Writers, pg. 63

6. Francis Schaeffer, Francis Schaeffer Trilogy: The God Who Is There, pg. 164

7. John MacArthur, The John MacArthur Bible Commentary, pg 1505

8. John MacArthur, The John MacArthur Bible Commentary, pg 1505

9. Edwin Orr, Playing the Good News Off Key, Christianity Today, January 1, 1982, pg. 27

10. Warren Wiersbe, The Wiersbe Bible Commentary: New Testament, pg. 87

11. R. Albert Mohler Jr., Holman Bible Dictionary, pg. 436

12. L. Paige Patterson, Holman Bible Dictionary, pg. 168

Chapter 5

The Purpose of the Church to Itself

*"The church is the gathering of God's children, where they
can be helped and fed like babies and then guided by her
motherly care, grow up to manhood in maturity of faith."*
- John Calvin

IN THE PREVIOUS chapters, we laid out the church's ultimate purpose in relation to God. We then explained the number one purpose of the church to the world. We're now going to look at the purpose of the church to itself which can be broken up into three facets: equipping, edifying, and encouraging the saints of God.

Edification

The word "edify" in the New Testament is translated from the Greek word *oikodomeo* (oy-kod-om-eh'-o) which means "to be a house builder or constructor." When used in reference to people, it means to build them up. Within the church, the ultimate goal of edification is to help someone become stronger in the faith.

As ye have therefore received Christ Jesus the Lord, so walk ye in him: Rooted and built up in him, and stablished in the faith, as ye have been taught, abounding therein with thanksgiving. (Colossians 2:6-7)

Edification is specifically given *to* the church *for* the church.

Wherefore comfort yourselves together, and edify one another, even as also ye do. (1 Thessalonians 5:11)

The way that the church is edified is through a number of ways. One is through spiritual gifts, especially those of the speaking kind (1 Corinthians 14). In this chapter, Paul lays out some very plain methods of edification of the church which includes elements of worship (1 Corinthians 14:26) and looking out for a weaker brother in Christ (Romans 15:1-2).

Equipping

This responsibility falls to the leaders in the church as their priority, though it is not something that is theirs exclusively. Commonly referred to as the five-fold ministry, it's a reflection on a church on how well they are equipped for full ministry so that they can live for God as the people of God. It is here that many churches around the world fail miserably. When the leaders of a church are more concerned with how entertained they can keep the congregation or with how many people they can draw to an event, we have a problem Houston.

Ephesians 4 gives a list of the different ministries that any healthy church will have to some degree or another. Though there are those who believe that some of these ministries have ceased, I will explain why I believe the scriptures say otherwise. Even so, the main point here is not whether or not the passage conveys this so much as whether or not the functions are being met in the church for the purpose of equipping.

As we begin this, we must be clear that no matter what side of the fence you're on, it's safe to say that they are given to the church as a gift from the Lord. Ephesians 4:7 says:

But unto every one of us is given grace according to the measure of the gift of Christ.

Dr. Wiersbe defines the gifts of these men as:

...a God-given ability to serve God and other Christians in such a way that Christ is glorified and believers edified.[1]

So the ultimate purpose of these gifts is in service to God and His church. It's in this context that we'll take a look at these gifted men and how each helps the church.

Apostles

Apostles (he that is sent or sent one) during the founding of the church were considered in one of two classes:

1. The twelve apostles who were specially chosen individuals who Christ hand-picked. In order to hold that office, the requirements were you have to have seen the risen Lord and that miracles were performed at the preaching of the word to confirm it (2 Corinthians 12:12, Hebrews 2:4). Their ministry was primarily founding and administering in the church as well as scriptural revelation. In this sense, there are no other apostles nor ever will be.

2. In a secondary sense, there were apostles that were sent to preach and help administer and form churches, what we today would know as missionaries or church planters. It is in this secondary sense that we look at those who are apostles today.

There are some in the body of Christ who have the giftedness to plant and nurture new churches on sound biblical doctrine. Once a church has been built up to a point where there are others to carry on the work in truth and the power of the Spirit, they move on to another place that God leads them to do the same thing while always having a special authority in the churches they have planted.

In a very broad sense, every Christian has an apostolic ministry because the Lord declared in John 20:21:

Peace be unto you: as my Father hath sent me, even so send I you.

Even so, not all men are gifted in the forming and administering of a church. Some are, and they aid in initiating a local body of believers into a cohesive family, making sure that there are others who will carry on the work in that body before they move on. If they are not doing this, it doesn't matter what they call themselves, they are not apostles in any sense, except in their imagination.

Prophets

This word conjures up images of a man standing on a mountain with a long gray beard with a staff like Charleton Heston in *The Ten Commandments*. They receive direct revelation from God, even secret, hidden things, which allowed them to foretell events and speak His word to the people, much of what was considered scripture. Though that may have been true from an Old Testament standpoint, that is not true from a New Testament standpoint.

The apostles' doctrine is what the foundation of the church was built upon (Acts 2:42). The apostles were the ones receiving revelation from God through the Holy Spirit on how Christ's church would be represented in the world. They, in a very literal sense, were the prophets of their day, much like the Old Testament.

New Testament prophets are cut from a slightly different cloth. They speak forth God's revelation in the same sense as Old Testament prophets but what they say is in line with the Scriptures. They're not propagating new revelation from God, especially that which contradicts the Bible. They can discern what specific word from the scriptures is needed for a specific person or body of believers and express this through inspired preaching. The crux of their ministry is not to foretell events or reveal secret things though this can and does happen. It is to speak forth God's specific word for a specific time that is in line or comes directly from the Scriptures. It's the right word at the right time for the right people.

Arguably, this is also a ministry for every believer for the Scriptures say to, "Preach the word in season and out of season (2 Timothy 4:2)." However, some have a gift for doing this consistently which encourages the church to know that God is directing them exactly where He wants them to go. This is why every church is not the same in operation or focus. New Testament prophets help crystallize the specifics.

Evangelists

Evangelists are those in the church who preach the good news of salvation. Dr. William McDonald's description is spot on:

They are divinely equipped to win the lost to Christ.

> They have the special ability to diagnose a sinner's
> condition, probe the conscience, answer objections,
> encourage decisions for Christ, and help the convert
> find assurance through the Word.[2]

The evangelists are the commanders in the salvation infantry so to speak. They have the spiritual insight to know where, when, and how to hit the unbeliever so that they can be set free. The church needs evangelists because they help the church grow.

Again, everyone in the church should be evangelizing as was mentioned in the last section. Every Christian has been given the ministry of reconciliation. As with the others, some have a special knack for doing it than others, a special aptitude given by God for His church. They reap souls more often than others.

Pastors

Many biblical scholars like to group pastors and teachers together as one but it doesn't appear to be in that vein in the context of what Paul is relaying. These men are given the consummate gifts to be able to perform the service in the church to which they were called. Not all pastors are teachers and vice versa. As Dr. McDonald points out:

> If pastors and teachers are the same person here in
> verse 11, then, by the same rule of grammar, so are
> apostles and prophets in [Ephesians] 2:20.[3]

Though the Greek grammar rule on that is clear of how the "and" is related when in the singular or plural, there seems to be only a correlation because of the service that pastors must do which is partly to teach. It's why in 1 Timothy 3:2, it gives the condition that a bishop should be apt to teach or able to give instruction. It doesn't mean that they are gifted teachers.

The word "pastor" is translated from the Greek *poimen* which literally means shepherd. In reference to the church, it's one who looks over the well-being of the flock of Christ, His church, with tender care. It's a service committed exclusively to elders and so is tied directly to it except that the pastor is a gifted individual while the elder is an office (though the term pastor is often used to mean elder). The function of elders is to pastor the flock of the Lord but some are more gifted than others. It's also used synonymously with overseer, bishop, and presbyter (interchanged in some translations).

It is thought in some Christian circles that the gift of pastor is the special sensitivity in some individuals to counsel, care, and aid believers in their growth in Christ. They are not necessarily dynamic individuals but are compassionate. They are person-oriented instead of task-oriented. They may not necessarily be a senior pastor of a church but a deacon or elder.

Teachers

This one I'm going to spend a little bit of time on since I have some experience here.

Teachers have been given spiritual insight into the scriptures and have the ability to convey this to church members so that they can learn and apply scriptural truths to their lives. They break down the Word of God so that people can understand and live it. It is a very grave responsibility to have in a church because the more one knows of the word of God, the more accountable they are held to it. That is why in James 3:1, the Bible says:

Be not many of you teachers, my brethren, knowing that we shall receive heavier judgment.

Teachers are not just able to instruct. They are blessed with an ability to instruct in a way where others will learn. That's the litmus test of a gifted teacher. People learn.

Now, it would seem that would be a given but you don't know how many people go to a church where someone is set up in a Bible study, Sunday school, or even the pulpit who has no clue what they're doing, let alone what they're talking about. This leaves those they are teaching just as clueless as when they came and they end up learning nothing. I have personally been in these situations on several occasions. On one occasion, it was so awful ,I had to leave the church because heresy was being taught by the senior pastor. It would have been wise for him to use the gifted teachers in the body to teach the congregation instead of believing that he had to do it all himself when he didn't take the requisite time to prepare.

I have to make a small interjection here on laboring in the Word, a discipline that is woefully lacking in the modern church . When I say laboring in the Word, that's exactly what I mean. It takes work to take out lexicons, dictionaries, commentaries, and other references to make sure that one is handling the word of God accurately and carefully. It is not enough to simply read some passages of scriptures, take a couple notes, then think that you're ready to teach something of lasting value. Since I'm a staunch believer in going through the scriptures line by line, it takes me several hours to study and write what needs to be conveyed so that my listeners will get the most out of the Scriptures. That means studying every single day. Study for Sunday starts Monday. As leaders in the church, we must give preeminence to the Word of the living God. We must have the attitude like the elders in Acts 6:2 who said:

And the twelve called the multitude of the disciples unto them, and said, It is not fit that we should forsake the word of God, and serve tables.

Leaders in the church today have forgotten the importance of sweating in the Word. Meetings have superseded the time that should be spent pouring over the Scriptures in order to properly feed the flock of Christ. To some degree, all leaders have the responsibility in this as was pointed out earlier in 2 Timothy 3:2. This is not an option. It is a duty. For those who are not particularly gifted as teachers, they should use those who are to help them. Too many times, pastors are expected to be Superman and they then give in to this fallacious notion instead of asking for help from other leaders who have the gift.

Can you tell I'm passionate about this?

For every one of these, no matter how you slice them up, the purpose is to use them for the benefit of others in the church so that they would mature in Christ. That is the goal. It's not about quantity, it's about quality.

Again, this is a responsibility that is not just for those that are gifted but for everyone that's a part of the church.

For when for the time ye ought to be teachers, ye have need that one teach you again which be the first principles of the oracles of God; and are become such as have need of milk, and not of strong meat. (Hebrews 5:12)

Encouragement

If edification is building the church up, encouragement is spurring it on. It means to give comfort or consolation. We are called to do all of it.

Expressed as a noun, the word is translated *paraklesis* which means "a calling to one's aid." Used as a verb (*protrepomai*) it means to counsel or advise. To urge forward. It's used interchangeably with the word "exhort" in the King James.

Encouraging doesn't just mean in the positive sense of comfort and strengthening. It's also used in the negative sense as warning, admonishing, or correcting. Dr. McDonald describes it as:

> ...stirring up saints to desist from every form of evil
> and press on to new achievements for Christ in holi-
> ness and in service.

The tragedy of the church today is that there are too many who are encouraging those in the church to live and be that which is contrary to the scriptures. Everything is allowed for the sake of tolerance. A new version of of the old antinomianism. Couple that with a blatant, woeful lack of church discipline and we have churches who run amuck, not following the dictates of scripture but of their own desires. What is right is not determined by sound biblical doctrine but the prevailing thinking of the day and how the people in the church feel. At no other time in history have we been able to clearly see the outworking of 1 Timothy 3:1-2.

Now the Spirit speaketh expressly, that in the latter times some shall depart from the faith, giving heed to seducing spirits, and doctrines of devils; Speaking lies in hypocrisy; having their conscience seared with a hot iron;

This should be a sign for the church to encourage each other more. Far too often, godly encouragement is left to just Sunday during the two to three hour spurt when we gather together. This is anathema to what the scriptures teach us.

*Not forsaking the assembling of ourselves together, as the manner of some is; but exhorting one another: **and so much the more** (emphasis mine), as ye see the day approaching. (Hebrews 10:25)*

The whole message of the gospel is an encouragement (as well as a command) to the world to turn to Christ and live. For the church, we encourage each other to stay and grow in Christ.

Edify, equip, and encourage the saints. This is the purpose of the church to itself. It's why the Lord built His church to exist here. However, this is separate and distinct from the purpose of why we gather together as His people.

Why the Church Gathers

As the church of the living God, His children which He has chosen, we gather for four major reasons: teaching, prayer, worship, and fellowship.

Teaching

In the book of Colossians, Paul encourages the Christian believers in Colosse to put on the new man and to grow in the character of holiness. One way this is done is through teaching:

Let the word of Christ dwell in you richly in all wisdom; teaching and admonishing one another in psalms and hymns and spiritual songs, singing with grace in your hearts to the Lord. (Colossians 3:16)

The purpose of the psalms and hymns is not as some form of entertainment. It is supposed to be used to teach and admonish (reprove mildly or warn against something). It is a method of solidifying the word of Christ within us. A song we will remember. What that song is saying and teaching is important because that's what's being deposited in our hearts and minds. In short, psalms, hymns, and spiritual songs are supposed to teach sound biblical doctrine and principles.

I am amazed today at what passes for Christian music. It doesn't have anything to do with musical styles as much as it has to do with what's being said in the song. Whether a musical artist believes it or not, when they write a song, they are teaching something, not just expressing themselves. A Christian who uses music as that means of expression has the responsibility to make sure that what they are teaching lines up with the word of God.

This goes even more so for the worship leader. A worship leader should have a sound understanding of the word of God. Much of the music that passes for worship in churches today talk more about ourselves than about God. If our music is to be worshipful, then the object of that worship should be the main focus.

Dr. Wiersbe writes:

There is (according to Paul) a definite relationship between our knowledge of the Bible and our expression of worship in song. One way we teach and encourage ourselves and others is through the singing of the Word of God. But if we do not know the Bible and understand it, we cannot honestly sing it from our hearts.[5]

Praying

In addition to teaching, the church gathers to pray.

Praying always with all prayer and supplication in the Spirit, and watching thereunto with all perseverance and supplication for all saints. (Ephesians 6:18)

Seek the LORD and his strength, seek his face continually. (1 Chronicles 16:11)

Prayer is the mortar of Christian faith. Praying for one another should be the normal business of the church. We pray for those who are suffering and in need, for favor, for strength, or whatever the situation calls for. If we know of a situation in someone's life, we shouldn't sit around gossiping or just talking about it as if that alone is the remedy. That's the world's way of doing things. We should entreat the God of the universe to intervene and change it for His glory.

Worship

A third element is worship and is the primary reason of the gathering of the church. This is not only through song as many people mistakenly believe. This is through an intimate time with the Father and is facilitated through His word, prayer, and a life of obedience. Though worship is personal and should be going on every day of our lives, when among the church a person's individual worship it is added in unity and unison to the corporate body of the household of God.

In addition, a part of corporate worship is administering the sacraments, specifically Communion or what's commonly referred to as the Lord's Supper, and baptism. These are specific aspects that are only for believers. Wayne Grudem explains this well:

> Groups who do not administer baptism and the Lord's Supper signify that they are not intending to function as a church. Someone may stand on a street corner with a small crowd and have a true preaching and hearing of the Word, but the people there would not be a church. Even a neighborhood Bible study meeting in a home can have the true teaching and hearing of the Word without becoming a church. But if a local Bible study began baptizing its own new con-

verts and regularly participating in the Lord's Supper, these things would signify an intention to function as a church and it would be difficult to say why it should not be considered a church in itself.[6]

Martin Luther, the great reformer, stated in the Augsburg Confession that a true church was:

The congregation of saints in which the gospel is rightly taught and the Sacraments rightly administered.[7]

The operative word there is "rightly". This is why many today who call themselves a church and administer the sacraments are not the true church of God. Mormons, who like to redefine themselves as the Church of Latter Day Saints, and Jehovah's Witnesses fall into this category as well as liberal Protestant churches who consistently tell their congregants that they can't trust the Bible. These are false churches and are recognized by orthodox Christianity as cults.

Fellowship

A fourth element is fellowship.

Behold, how good and how pleasant it is for brethren to dwell together in unity! (Psalm 133:1)

Many churches have a main meeting just once a week which is normally on Sunday. The majority of our time is spent away from the strong company of other Christians that is found in the church. For those six days of the week that we have to spend in the world dealing with the flesh, the world, and the devil, we have to be encouraged to deal with this in the way that God would want us to deal with it. When we gather with our church, we have the opportunity to directly seek Godly counsel on a plethora of life issues.

The Bible declares:

Where no counsel is, the people fall: but in the multitude of counsellors there is safety. (Proverbs 11:14)

Hear counsel, and receive instruction, that thou mayest be wise in thy latter end. (Proverbs 19:20)

The church should be a haven where godly advice and encouragement should be in abundant supply at all times. This is not just from the pastor but from the many Godly men and women who serve the Lord and whose lives reflect this.

Being around other believers should bring joy to the Christian's heart. The Spirit that lives within us moves among us when we fellowship. However, fellowship is more than just "hanging out" and having some talk time while we eat (discussed in Chapter 2). Suffice it to say that a basic understanding of fellowship as a bond is exclusively between Christians.

These elements should be present when the church gathers and should be the focus of our gathering. It's important to keep these things in mind as we move along because this is part of the basis for presenting a mindset that we should stop bringing unbelievers to our church gatherings.

References

1. Warren Wiersbe, The Wiersbe Bible Commentary: New Testament, pg. 606

2. William MacDonald, The Believer's Bible Commentary, pg 1935

3. William MacDonald, The Believer's Bible Commentary, pg 1935

4. William MacDonald, The Believer's Bible Commentary, pg 1730

5. Warren Wiersbe, The Wiersbe Bible Commentary: New Testament, pg. 688

6. Wayne Grudem, Systematic Theology, pg. 866

7. Augsburg Confession, Article 7

Interlude

The Unbeliever and the Church

"I believe that there are too many practitioners in the church, who are not believers." - C.S. Lewis

IN CHAPTER 5, I explained what the purpose of the church was in gathering together. In summary, they were teaching, prayer, worship, and fellowship. What the next chapter will present is how an unbeliever has no part in any of those as they function in the church and how the unbeliever's condition causes them to run counter to those purposes. By understanding this, we'll be able to understand how we are to relate to them in a way that is loving and wise.

The idea of inviting unbelievers to a church gathering is wholly unbiblical. It was not something that was even thought of in the early church. In *Christian Liturgy: Catholic and Evangelical*, Frank Senn notes:

> So far as we know, the public was not invited. Newcomers, seekers, strangers, and visitors had to be vouched for by sponsors. In fact, early Christian writers were at pains to point out the differences between their assemblies and the pagan cults. This indicates that the ritual bareness of early Christian worship should not be taken as a sign of primitiveness, but rather as a way of emphasizing the spiritual character of Christian worship.[1]

In other words, inviting unbelievers to church didn't come from a biblical mandate. It came from pagan practice. One of the ways we try to cover this up is by saying we need to be "relevant."

It's important to understand what is meant by "unbeliever." It means someone who has not repented of their sins and is still in a state of rebellion against God. It has nothing to do with how moral, kind, or nice they are. They are individuals still under the wrath of God.

In what is arguably the most famous sermon given by an American preacher, Jonathan Edwards expounds on the sinner's condition in *Sinners in the Hands of an Angry God:*

> The God who holds you over the pit of hell, as one
> might hold a spider or some loathsome insect over the
> fire, abhors you and is dreadfully provoked. His wrath
> toward you burns like fire; He looks upon you as
> worth of nothing else but to be cast into the fire. His
> eyes are so pure that He cannot bear to have you in His
> sight; you are ten thousand times more abominable
> in His eyes than the most hateful, venomous serpent
> is in ours.[2]

Unbelievers are under the wrath of God and daily build up
wrath in disobedience. Symbolically, they are the unclean donkey,
stubborn and obstinate in its ways, concerned only with what it
wants and not what its master wants from them. In their current
state, they have nothing to look forward to from God but judgment,
damnation, and hell. It is in this condition that believers bring them
into a church gathering.

Having understood this, let's now turn to each individual
aspect of the church gathering and lay out why the unbeliever has
no part in any of it.

References

1. Frank. C Senn, Christian Liturgy: Catholic and Evangelical, pg. 53

2. Jonathan Edwards, Sinners In the Hands of An Angry God, pg. 39-40

Chapter 6

Why We Should Stop Bringing Them to Church

"If we fail to exclude unbelievers from the fellowship of the body we're in error. The church isn't designed for unbelievers to come and say whatever they want and be accepted as they are." - John MacArthur

IN CHAPTER 5, it was presented what should happen in the midst of the gathering of the church. Four aspects were delineated: teaching, prayer, worship and fellowship. We'll now take a look at each one closely and explain how the unbeliever is fully incapable of being a part of each.

Teaching - Unable to Hear

Unbelievers are spiritually deaf. It was one of the reasons why our Lord spoke in parables.

Therefore speak I to them in parables: because they seeing see not; and hearing they hear not, neither do they understand. (Matthew 13:13)

He that hath ears to hear, let him hear. (Matthew 11:15)

This last verse is a call to pay attention very closely because what was being said was of profound and deep significance. It was a call to understand and believe. The saying infers that everyone doesn't have ears to hear. This is the state of the unbeliever. They do not have the ability to hear because their spiritual ears are plugged.

And he said, Go and tell this people, hear ye indeed but understand not; and see ye indeed but perceive not. Make the heart of this people fat and make their ears heavy, and shut their eyes; lest they see with their eyes and hear with their ears and understand with their hearts and convert, and be healed. (Isaiah 6:10)

Unbelievers are in a state of willful rebellion against God. They have no interest in God's word, His ways, or in God Himself. They set themselves up in array against Him. God and His word are not something pleasing to them but something that's offense to them.

*To whom shall I speak, and give warning, that they may hear? behold, their ear is uncircumcised, and they **cannot** (emphasis mine) hearken: behold, the word of the LORD is unto them a reproach; they have no delight in it. (Jeremiah 6:10)*

Unbelievers cannot hear because they do not have the capacity to. Spiritually, they are dead men walking and so the teaching that comes forth in a sermon is incomprehensible because they are still carnal. This was alluded to in the Jeremiah 6:10 passage and is stated plainly in Paul's first letter to the Corinthians.

*But the natural man receiveth not the things of the Spirit of God: for they are foolishness unto him: **neither** <u>can</u> **he know them** (emphasis mine), because they are spiritually discerned. (1 Corinthians 2:14)*

Intellectually it may be there but spiritually they are blinded and in outright rebellion to what they do pick up. It is important to understand that more knowledge about the Bible does not make an unbeliever a true Christian. It never does and in many cases it hardens their hearts even more. It gives them just enough information to damn them. This was the case with the Pharaoh in the book of Exodus who knew that God was bringing the plagues but refused to capitulate. More knowledge about God only further damned him. It's not a matter of knowledge. It's a matter of submission.

The hope that many have is that somehow a biblical teaching will turn on the light bulb for their friend or loved one that they bring into a church gathering. But it's God that turns on the light bulb that gives them the capacity to understand, not the teaching. If teaching alone could somehow make men saved, there would be many more Christians on earth. But that's not the case because a teaching alone will not turn on the light for them . It is the Holy Spirit which opens the ears and hearts of a spiritually blind and deaf individual, who uses godly teaching or preaching as a conduit to where they can understand and discern the truth. He empowers them to hear, understand, and believe. If the Holy Spirit has not arrested their heart and brought them to a state of repentance before Christ, they may as well be watching a foreign film without subtitles. They hear but don't understand. What they do understand they won't obey rightly because they do not have the Holy Spirit nor the righteousness of Christ imputed to them which means whatever righteousness they perform in relation to currying God's acceptance is as filthy rags and useless.

Prayer - Unheard and Offensive

I had a young man come to me and ask me about his aunt who was an unbeliever. She had won some money gambling and he said she prayed for it. When I told him that God didn't hear her prayers, he looked at me puzzled. What he had deduced in his mind was that since she got what she prayed for, her prayers had been answered. However, after going through the scriptures, he understood that it had nothing to do with her prayers.

So what happens when an unbeliever prays and what they pray comes to pass? Several things could be happening. Primarily, it has to do with God's sovereign will. Or it could be another saint praying on their behalf. Rest assured, it has nothing to do with their prayers at all.

The believer is the only one who has the privilege of approaching God in this way.

Let us therefore come boldly unto the throne of grace, that we may obtain mercy, and find grace to help in time of need. (Hebrews 4:16)

For where two or three are gathered together in my name, there am I in the midst of them. (Matthew 18:20)

In the Matthew 18:20 passage, though the context is speaking about discipline in the church, the clause itself is not exclusive to just disciplinary action. The phrase "in my name" means under the authority of Christ as if He is making the appeal Himself. When Jesus is the center of the gathering, He is there. The child of God realizes this and is able to approach God through the shed blood of Christ. They have the right to petition the Lord with supplications and requests at any time because they have come under His authority.

The unbeliever, however, has no such privilege since they have not put themselves under the authority of Christ. As a matter of fact, their prayers are not heard at all.

If I regard iniquity in my heart, the Lord will not hear me: (Psalm 66:18)

But your iniquities have separated between you and your God, and your sins have hid his face from you, that he will not hear. (Isaiah 59:2)

He that turneth away his ear from hearing the law, even his prayer shall be abomination. (Proverbs 28:9)

In the Old Testament, the altar of incense in the tabernacle was a symbol of the prayers of the saints reaching up to God which is reiterated in Revelation 8:3-4. The incense that was to be offered was of a particular blend and it was supposed to be most holy and pure. They were not to use it for any other purpose (Exodus 30:34-38).

Earlier in that same chapter, the Lord gives instruction on the building of the incense altar and commands Israel not to offer any strange incense on it (Exodus 30:1-9). The word "strange" is translated from the Hebrew *zur* which means "to be a foreign or profane." Any other incense that was offered that was not of the specific kind that the Lord prescribed was considered profane, unholy, and unusable in service to Him. As a matter of fact, the high priest at the time, Aaron, had two sons who also ministered as priests, Nadab and Abihu. The Lord killed them because they offered strange fire on the altar which ties directly to having strange incense (Leviticus 10:1-3).

In addition, the blood sacrifice was tied to the burning of

incense as theologians Karl Keil and Franz Delitzsch explain:

> ...the connection between the incense-offering and the burnt-offering is indicated by the rule that they were to be offered at the same time. Both offerings shadowed forth the devotion of Israel to its God, whilst the fact that they were offered every day exhibited this devotion as constant and uninterrupted. But the distinction between them consisted in this, that in the burnt or whole offering Israel consecrated and sanctified its whole life and action in both body and soul to the Lord, whilst in the incense-offering its prayer was embodied as the exaltation of the spiritual man to God.[1]

Since an unbeliever has not turned from their wickedness and renounced the ways of the world, turning to the Lord as their Savior and coming under His authority, the sin that they live in and perpetrate blocks any prayer from being heard. Their prayers are "foreign" in that they are not offered in direct connection with the blood sacrifice of the Lord Jesus Christ or His righteousness. James declares that the effectual and fervent prayer of a righteous man availeth much (James 5:15). But the righteousness that we have must be imputed to us from God through the Lord Jesus Christ (Romans 4:23-25).

When an unbeliever prays, they are approaching God on their

own righteousness and not through the righteousness of Christ. That they should approach God in their own self-righteousness, which to God is as filthy rags (Isaiah 64:6), is just more sin being perpetrated and the Lord God wholly rejects. In this state, unbelievers have no business joining in with the church in solemn prayer to God. The only prayer that God will hear from an unbeliever is along the lines of, "I repent. Forgive and have mercy on me Lord."

Fellowship - Unequally Yoked

2 Corinthians 6:14 says:

Be ye not unequally yoked together with unbelievers: for what fellowship hath righteousness with unrighteousness? and what communion hath light with darkness?

A yoke is a wooden frame that was put around the necks of animals such as oxen, donkeys, or horses. A basic yoke has a bar and two loops made of either rope or wood that goes around the animal's neck. There are more elaborate ones made of leather and are one whole unit. Their purpose is to make sure that the animals pull in tandem.

In the Old Testament, the Lord forbade the children of Israel to mix animals in their plowing.

Thou shalt not plow with an ox and an ass together. (Deuteronomy 22:10)

The reason for this was twofold.

The first was that one animal was clean and the other unclean. Israel was to be an example of God's holiness in everything, even a small thing like plowing.

The second is that they couldn't pull in tandem. The animals had two different temperaments and gaits and would be unable to plow in a straight line which was necessary for proper planting. In this we see God's love taking care of His people in even the smallest things, in addition to taking care of his creation since this would put undue stress and discomfort on the animals. But more so, it's an example of God's holiness and how He expects His people to be holy in the smallest of things (Leviticus 22:18).

2 Corinthians 6:14 is almost exclusively used in speaking of marriage relationships in modern day Christianity. Though this definitely applies to that, it's not the only kind of relationship that the apostle Paul is talking about here and actually is not the primary idea he had mind.

The word "fellowship" is the Greek word *metoche* which means participation or intercourse. It's derived from the root meaning of *metecho* which means belong to. He's speaking of being tied closely with unbelievers in any way. This extends to business relationships, clubs, and most definitely, the church where there is a spiritual tie or yoking that is being expressed in the relation of the church body. This yoking is culminated in the sacrament of the Lord's Supper. Paul warns in 1 Corinthians 11:29 that he who eats and drinks of the Lord's table unworthily or unfit is bringing damnation to themselves and relates that directly to sickness and death in the church. Unbelievers are wholly unfit to partake at the Lord's table at all.

Believers have true fellowship only with the church made up of saints alone, and by extension, unbelievers have no business in the church for this reason. They have not been redeemed, they are still in rebellion to God, and thus they should not be welcomed as equals into the fellowship of any local church or into the church universal.

No where is this seen most clearly then in the parable of the wedding banquet in Matthew 22:11. Here, God began inviting outsiders, the Gentiles, of whom some were of high estate to the most degenerate. This is representative of His church. However, there was one among them that did not have on the proper wedding garment. In other words, they didn't belong. They weren't saved and had no business among His people. They were put out of the feast and cast into the place where they belonged which was the outer darkness.

The book of Amos says:

Can two walk together except they be agreed? (Amos 3:3)

The question, of course, is rhetorical and requires the answer "No." So why then are Christians all around the world bringing unbelievers into the fellowship of saints who are yoked first to Christ and then to each other alone? Why are they yoking themselves to unbelievers spiritually by bringing unbelievers into the congregation of the saints to join in on something that they have no right to be a part of whatsoever, which is the gathering of the church?

A big part of this is a misconception of what love is. We believe that since the Lord ate with sinners and tax collectors, those who were considered the detritus of society, we should accept any and all into the church. There are a couple of problems with this line of thinking.

The first problem is that it doesn't reflect what Jesus was doing. At all. The Lord was providing an example that we should follow. He was going out to them, not waiting for them to come to Him. As mentioned in the previous chapter, part of the mission of the church is to go.

For the Son of man is come to seek and to save that which was lost. (Luke 19:10)

Second, the main reason for going is because man does not seek after God by his own volition and desire and therefore, wouldn't go looking for Him (Psalm 14:2-3).

Third, He was not gathering with the church but was evangelizing the lost. The church had not even been founded. There were occasions where He gathered with those who were His true disciples exclusively, separating from the multitude. During these times,

He would give them information that He wouldn't give others. He had set it aside solely for them. This happened on more than one occasion, most markedly the institution of the Last Supper (Matthew 26:20-30) among others (Matthew 13:11-13, Mark 13:3-5, Luke 10:23-24).

In reality, it's not love that motivates us to bring people to church but disobedience in spreading the gospel and ignorance of God's word.

Worship – Corrupt and Insincere

There is a story that's told of a man who had a dream where he was escorted by an angel to a church gathering. It was a familiar scene. The people were clapping with enthusiasm and raising their hands while others were reading from their hymnals. The pianist was playing with fervency while the drummer was banging away. The choir was swaying back and forth in tandem. After they were finished, the preacher got up and began to speak. He walked back and forth across the stage, pointing, pounding his fist on the podium, using his arms to speak.

As all of this is going on, the man noticed the most peculiar thing. There was absolutely no sound. Not a decibel. Perplexed by all this, the man turned to the angel.

"I don't understand. Why can't I hear anything?"

"You cannot hear anything because there is nothing to hear.

These people may look like they are worshiping the Lord God, but in reality their hearts are far from from Him. This is what we hear in heaven and it happens every Sunday."

The Bible says in John 4:24:

God is a Spirit: and they that worship him must worship him in spirit and in truth.

Worship without repentance is idolatry and an abomination to God. It is false worship and pretentious, empty religion. It's put on for show only and God does not accept it.

Dr. William McDonald explains:

> There must be no sham or hypocrisy. There must be no pretense to being religious when inwardly one's life is corrupt. There must be no idea that in going through a series of rituals, God is thereby pleased. Even if God instituted those rituals Himself, He still insists that man approach Him with a broken and contrite heart.[2]

This, of course, is not possible for an unbeliever because they are not capable of worshiping in the way that God would accept because they do not have the Spirit of God in them. The Holy Spirit is the definer of whether someone is saved and once a believer is indwelt by His presence, He leads and guides with the correct attitude and life making it possible for proper worship. In contrast, this is absolutely impossible for an unbeliever, for it says in Romans 8:9:

But ye are not in the flesh, but in the Spirit, if so be that the Spirit of God dwell in you. Now if any man have not the Spirit of Christ, he is none of his.

Man's religion is worthless. It is an attempt to appease God not with sincere faith and a pure heart but external works. This doesn't please God in the least.

For they being ignorant of God's righteousness, and going about to establish their own righteousness, have not submitted themselves unto the righteousness of God. (Romans 10:3)

But without faith it is impossible to please him: for he that cometh to God must believe that he is, and that he is a rewarder of them that diligently seek him. (Hebrews 11:6)

False worship in this sense is self-centered. It's not done out of adoration and faith towards God, but to be seen as pious. It is the religion of the Pharisees which the Lord condemned as hypocrisy on many occasions. It is an offense for unbelievers to be with God's saints in insincere worship.

There are two portions of scripture where this is presented.

The first is in Deuteronomy 23:1-4.

He that is wounded in the stones, or hath his privy member cut off, shall not enter into the congregation of the LORD. A bastard shall not enter into the congregation of the LORD; even to his tenth generation shall he not enter into the congregation of the LORD. An Ammonite or Moabite shall not enter into the congregation of the LORD; even to their tenth generation shall they not enter into the congregation of the LORD for ever: Because they met you not with bread and with water in the way, when ye came forth out of Egypt; and because they hired against thee Balaam the son of Beor of Pethor of Mesopotamia, to curse thee.

Someone who was a eunuch was not allowed into the congregation. This bodily mutilation was a defect that detracted from the natural order that God had created. God's people were to be holy and as the sacrifices, without blemish. We, as the church of God, are to be without blemish also. We should present ourselves as living sacrifices. This cannot be done without the blood of Christ which cleanses us from all unrighteousness and unholiness, presenting us righteous and holy before God.

Second, those who were bastards were not allowed. The word "bastard" is translated from the Hebrew *mamzer* which means "a child from a Jewish and heathen union. " In this case, it may also refer to offspring from an incestuous or adulterous Jewish relationship. They were children who were born in a way that did not reflect the holiness of God and were a stigma in the community. Again, they were a symbol of how things were performed outside of God's divine order. Therefore, they were excluded unto the tenth generation, ten meaning completely, never having a chance.

This is analogous to the illegitimacy of those who try to

approach God outside of Christ instead of the way He wants to be approached. It's the thief and the robber that tries to come in by another way instead of the way that God has prescribed (John 10:21). Every way that doesn't come in by the way of Christ is illegitimate. Mormonism, Jehovah's Witnesseses, New Age spirituality, or even moral living by works.

Lastly was the Ammonites and the Moabites. Three reasons are given for their exclusion. First was because they opposed Israel and were their enemies. They instigated the cursing of Balaam on Israel and therefore brought a curse upon themselves (Genesis 12:3). Next, they were unrepentant, idolatrous pagans. Lastly, they were born out of incestuous relationships (Genesis 19:30-38).

The next portion recounts one of the numerous times when Israel had fallen away from God. How reflective it is of our time today is scary.

And thou shalt say to the rebellious, even to the house of Israel, Thus saith the Lord GOD; O ye house of Israel, let it suffice you of all your abominations, In that ye have brought into my sanctuary strangers, **uncircumcised in heart, and uncircumcised in flesh, to be in my sanctuary, to pollute it** *(emphasis mine), even my house, when ye offer my bread, the fat and the blood, and they have broken my covenant because of all your abominations. And ye have not kept the charge of mine holy things: but ye have set keepers of my charge in my sanctuary for* *yourselves. Thus saith the Lord GOD; No stranger, **uncircumcised in heart**, nor uncircumcised in flesh, **shall enter into my sanctuary, of any stranger that is among the children of Israel**. (Ezekiel 44:6-9)*

As we had seen in the Deuteronomy, the law prohibited foreigners from being admitted into the congregation of Israel unless certain requirements were met and even then it was limited. Being circumcised in the flesh was supposed to reflect outwardly that they were identifying with the God of Abraham, Isaac, and Jacob as a sign of the righteousness of faith they were supposed to have already inwardly. In many respects, it is similar to baptism in the church today. However, just as baptism does not save anyone, neither did being circumcised in the flesh mean that you were one of God's people. There must also be circumcision in the heart as well. Paul talks about this is Romans 2:

For he is not a Jew, which is one outwardly; neither is that circumcision, which is outward in the flesh: But he is a Jew, which is one inwardly; and circumcision is that of the heart, in the spirit, and not in the letter; whose praise is not of men, but of God. (Romans 2:28-29)

What Paul was saying was that outward circumcision of the flesh was only valid when it was combined with the sincerity and purity of inward circumcision of the heart . This manifested itself in fidelity to God through holy living and love for others according to God's law. Only then were you considered a true Jew or, in this explanation, a true child of God whose praise is from God. This is identically true for baptism as well.

The Ezekiel passage is God saying this. This was not only for those who were foreigners in a literal sense, but foreigners in a spiritual sense as well though they may have been a part of national Israel.

It reminds me of a story that I heard recounted by Dr. John MacArthur. He was at a pastors' conference teaching on elders. Afterward, a pastor came up to him and stated, "You know, I think I know what's wrong with my church. Half of the elders are saved and the other half unsaved."

I'd say that's just a wee bit of a problem.

We bring unsaved, unregenerate, unholy, unbelieving people into the congregation who have no desire to repent and then wonder why we have all of these problems in the church. Then believers get part of their influence from the pulpit and part from these same church attending unbelievers. If both sides of that coin is infected, there is mad trouble in River City.

Ultimately, God's enemies, those not in Christ, have no place in the congregation of His saints because their hearts are not right towards Him. The privilege of fellowship is not extended to unbelievers. It's extended to believers, penitent sinners, and that exclusively. Those who have life have nothing in common with those who are dead. A.W. Tozer put it well:

An organization and a name do not make a church.
One hundred religious persons knit into a unity by
careful organizations do not constitute a church any
more than eleven dead men make a football team.

The first requisite is life, always.[3]

In summary, the unbeliever is dull of hearing, their prayers
are not heard, they cannot have true fellowship with believers,
and are not capable of worshiping in Spirit and in truth which is
the only worship God accepts. This is because the church is not for
people in rebellion. It's for people who have laid down their arms
and surrendered to the lordship of Christ. It's not for those who
are dead in sins but for those who are alive in the righteousness of
Christ by the Holy Spirit of God. It's not for practicing sinners, but
for sinners no longer practicing.

References

1. Keil & Delitzch Commentary on the Old Testament, Leviticus 10:1-3
2. William MacDonald, The Believer's Bible Commentary, pg 1486
3. A.W. Tozer, Man-The Dwelling Place of God, Chapter 19

Chapter 7

For the Sake of Love

"When we love our fellow man for his own sake, the life of God flows through us, and when we are responsive to the God of Infinite Wisdom and Love, we are better able to discover and foster the moral and spiritual capacities of our fellow men." - E.W. Lyman

ALL THAT HAS been said thus far has been to drive home the reality of the biblical foundation of why we, as Christ's church, should stop bringing unbelievers into the midst of our worship gatherings. In a perfect world, we could end the matter there because obeying the Bible alone should be enough. Our attitude should be, "If the Bible says it, that's the end of it." Though that may be a simplified presentation, it's an attitude that more Christians should cultivate. However, this is not a perfect or simple world and there are more than a fair share of people who will read this book and disagree with what I've said, which is to be expected.

When we get down to brass tacks, the ultimate reason that we should stop bringing unbelievers to church is because of love. Love for the unbeliever. Love for the church. Love for God.

Love for the Unbeliever

There are several practical realities that we often forget when bringing unbelievers to church, the foremost being that it's not loving towards them. It puts the unbeliever in an awkward position. They are in a totally foreign environment with no way of acclimating because they do not have the Holy Spirit of God. It forces them into an impossible situation and very often ends up alienating them even more from wanting to become a part of the church.

In addition, it may lead to false conversion. Though they feel out of place, some people have a knack for fitting in. Saying the right phrases, acting the right way. Since someone has brought them to church instead of bringing them to Christ, others are fooled into believing that they are saved. This can go on for years with that individual truly believing that by doing the proper works and saying the right things, they are saved.

I'm reminded of the story of the late Dr. D. James Kennedy when he first met his wife. She had been in a Presbyterian church for a decade when he met her. However, after closer observation, it was apparent that she didn't know Christ. He ended up giving her the gospel and she became genuinely saved as a result. But for years she was simply a false convert. She had put on a cloak of religion and was able to function in the church in that capacity for a long time.

As we bring unbelievers to church, we potentially partake in building their disingenuous, false faith. We may ignorantly help in that individual's self-deception which is not just unloving but downright sinful. Our focus should not be to get them into the church. Our focus should be getting Christ into them. Only then will they be fit to gather with His church when they are genuinely covered by His blood.

Love for the Church

Since impenitent unbelievers have no desire for God, His way, or His truth, they become nothing but an obstacle in the church. They effectively become the enemy within. Paul warns us about this in his letter to the Corinthians and the Galatians:

Be not deceived: Evil companionships corrupt good morals. (1 Corinthians 15:33)

A little leaven leaveneth the whole lump. (Galatians 5:9)

Leaven was a small part of fermented dough in the making of bread that was used to ferment other dough. In the New Testament, it is often a symbol of sin or corruption. This is also reflected in the Old Testament in the Feast of Unleavened Bread.

Unbelievers in the church are spiritual leaven, a virus waiting to spread. They are a bad influence on the congregation of the saints. They bring in a conscience that is not controlled by the Holy Spirit but controlled by the flesh full of pride, envy, and a host of other undesirable things. Their worldview is secular in that it promotes the things of the flesh and not the things of the Spirit. Their hearts have not been captivated by the word of God but rejects it. Some of them are deadly like Hymenaeus, Alexander, or Diotrephes who come into the church causing problems on all kinds of levels for their own selfish ambition (1 Timothy 1:20, 3 John 9). Others take time to spread their poison, little by little.

It may seem rather harsh to think of unbelievers in such intense terms. Yet, the Bible is clear that unbelievers are building up wrath for themselves every day and that they are in rebellion to God (Romans 2:8). They are the children of disobedience (Ephesians 2:2) and it is this same disobedience to God's way that He warns us not to be ensnared by (Deuteronomy 12:30, 2 Peter 3:17). When we stop bringing them to church, we are protecting the church from their evil influence.

Protection of the church is partly the responsibility of the elders also. This is through church discipline. People are to be confronted with their sin in the church and put out when they refuse to repent (1 Corinthians 5:1-5, Titus 3:10). However, this is a rarity today as churches are more concerned with how many people are a part of their congregation rather than if the people in the congregation are actually saved and equipped for the work of the ministry. The holiness of God's church is not a priority but takes a back seat to tradition, programs, and false progress through numbers.

There is a story in the book of Joshua that illustrates the destructiveness of sin among God's people and the need for swift discipline. In chapter 7, the Israelites go to conquer the city of Ai. The Lord had warned them that when they went out to defeat their enemies, they were not supposed to touch the graven images or the silver and gold on them because they would be a snare unto them (Deuteronomy 7:25-26). However, Achan had taken material from the battle of Jericho. When they attempted to conquer the next city, Ai, they were defeated. Joshua didn't understand why but the Lord had revealed to Him that Israel had sinned. They could not get victory until the sin had been dealt with and eliminated.

This is a problem with far too many churches today. Sin is openly tolerated because of the wrong focus or because no one wants to offend anyone. In the process they end up offending God. I have personally been in churches where pre-marital sex was apparent because the couple kept having kids. No one said a word to that couple and now that church is trumpeting a spiritual dirge for itself because of disobedience and a failure to deal with sin in the church.

Protecting the church all goes back to having a love for the church to begin with. We should seek to do good to all, especially the household of faith (Galatians 6:10). Our actions should be predicated on the word of God because then we know that our actions are based on true love. When we bring unbelievers into the church, we think that we are being loving to the unbeliever when in truth, we are not. We are being unloving to both the unbeliever and the church in one fell swoop. What is loving to the unbeliever is to bring them to Christ by giving them the gospel and praying for them. What is loving to the church is to stop bringing unbelievers into the worship gatherings, protecting her from their evil influence and dealing with sin when it rears its head.

Love for the Lord

More than anything, we should stop bringing unbelievers to church because of a love for the Lord. Unbelievers in the midst of

His people perpetrating false worship is an affront to the Lord. He recognizes it for what it is: a cloak of self-piety wrapped in a covering of false religion.

But to the wicked God says: "What right have you to recite my statutes or take my covenant on your lips? For you hate discipline, and you cast my words behind you...These things you have done, and I have been silent; you thought that I was one like yourself. But now I rebuke you and lay the charge before you. (Psalms 50:16, 17, 21 ESV)

Insincere faith and false religion do not fool the Lord. He makes it clear that they have no right to even let His word and covenants fall from their lips because they themselves are an abomination through the corruptness of their hearts and the disobedience which they persist in.

In the book of Amos, He declares:

I hate, I despise your feasts, and I take no delight in your solemn assemblies. Even though you offer me your burnt offerings and grain offerings, I will not accept them; and the peace offerings of your fattened animals, I will not look upon them. Take away from me the noise of your songs; to the melody of your harps I will not listen. (Amos 5:21-23 ESV)

This kind of empty formalism with no true faith, no changed heart, no inner humility towards God, is a stench in His nostrils. Keil & Delitzsch note:

> ..the divine discourse is now turned to another class,
> viz., to the evil-doers, who, in connection with open

and manifest sins and vices, take the word of God upon their lips, a distinct class from those who base their sanctity upon outward works of piety, who out-wardly fulfill the commands of God, but satisfy and deceive themselves with this outward observance.[1]

This is not a small thing. This is not just unbelievers hurting themselves but it is sinful and evil in the sight of God.

Keep thy foot when thou goest to the house of God, and be more ready to hear, than to give the sacrifice of fools: for they consider not that they do evil. (Ecclesiastes 5:1)

Sin grieves the Spirit of God. As God's children, we do not want to grieve Him by facilitating false faith expressing itself in false worship from an unregenerate unbeliever who then infects His people. Dr. McDonald makes an observation of the reasons why we should not grieve the Holy Spirit:

1. He is the Holy Spirit. Anything that is not holy is distasteful to Him.

2. He is the Holy Spirit of God, a member of the blessed Trinity.

3. We were sealed by Him for the day of redemption....a seal speaks of ownership and security. He is the seal that guarantees our preservation until Christ returns for us and our salvation is complete.[2]

We show love towards God when we show love towards His people.

And the King shall answer and say unto them, Verily I say unto you, Inasmuch as ye have done it unto one of the least of these my brethren, ye have done it unto me. (Matthew 25:40)

Jonathan Edwards paints a graphic picture of just how offensive it is to the Lord:

> You have offended Him infinitely more than ever a stubborn rebel did his prince; and yet, it is nothing but His hand that holds you from falling into the fire every moment. There is no other reason to be given why you did not go to hell the moment you walked into the house of God on a Sunday morning, provoking His pure eyes by your sinful, wicked manner of attending his solemn worship.[3]

In Numbers 25, there was an incident where the Israelites had sunk into idolatry and performed idol worship because of the introduction of unbelievers in their midst. The Lord's edict was to slay all those who had apostatized and joined themselves to Baal of Peor, the false god of the Moabites. As a result, God had struck them with a plague that was moving throughout the camp. It was so bad that one of the leaders had paraded his pagan wife in the midst of them and took her into his home, displaying his sin flagrantly as if nothing was wrong while others were weeping at the door of the tabernacle praying for God's mercy. Upon seeing this, Phinehas, the son of Eleazar, took a javelin and ran them both through and as a result, stopped the plague.

We read this story today and think that it was a barbaric and violent thing that was done. But God saw it quite differently.

And the LORD spake unto Moses, saying, Phinehas, the son of Eleazar, the son of Aaron the priest, hath turned my wrath away from the children of Israel, while he was zealous for my sake among them, that I consumed not the children of Israel in my jealousy. Wherefore say, Behold, I give unto him my covenant of peace: And he shall have it, and his seed after him, even the covenant of an everlasting priesthood; because he was zealous for his God, and made an atonement for the children of Israel (Numbers 25:10-13).

God did not see this as an act of barbarism or murder. He saw this as an act of zeal and love for Himself and therefore blessed him. Some of the more radical and shocking actions by the people of God throughout history have proven to be the most courageous and godly undertakings. I say that because what I'm advocating may seem foolish and radical to the traditionally entrenched but I'm arguing that it is because of a zeal and love for God and His church that this has been written.

Though it may go against our traditional morays or flawed sensibilities, when we stop bringing unbelievers to church, we demonstrate our love and fidelity towards God.

References

1. Keil & Delitzch Commentary on the Old Testament, Psalm 50:16-21, paragraph 1.

2. William MacDonald, The Believer's Bible Commentary, pg 1940

3. Jonathan Edwards, Sinners In the Hands of An Angry God, pg. 40

Chapter 8

No Body's Perfect

A man is reported to have approached Charles Spurgeon looking for the perfect church. Spurgeon replied, "My church is not the one you're looking for. But if you should happen to find such a church, I beg you not to join it, for it would spoil the whole thing."

"Before Christ comes, it is useless to expect to see the perfect church." - John C. Ryle

IN READING THIS, I can almost guarantee that there will be someone who will get the wrong idea and think that

I'm propagating some kind of perfect, flawless church. That could not be further from the truth. The fact of the matter is as long there are unglorified human beings in the church here on earth, it will never be perfect. To think otherwise is to be living in a grand delusion.

There is no perfect, flawless church because there are no perfect, flawless human beings. The only One who accomplished such a task sits as reigning King in heaven and we now serve Him. We struggle and fail in our battle with the flesh. As Paul said in his letter to the church at Rome:

For that which I do I allow not: for what I would, that do I not; but what I hate, that do I. (Romans 7:15)

However, this is not to say that we don't press on in our walk with the Lord. On the contrary, we run the race to win. We don't make excuses for sin but day by day we submit to God and allow him to take hold of us more and more. We are never sinless but if we are truly walking with the Lord, we should be sinning less.

There are signs and general indicators that give us a pretty good idea of who the legit Christians are. For the most part, we know our own. However, membership in a local church does not mean automatic entrance into heaven. Paul mentions this in Romans 9 in speaking of Israel:

Not as though the word of God hath taken none effect. For they are not all Israel, which are of Israel: (Romans 9:6)

The same can be said today: For they are not all of the church who are among the church. People can perform all of the right religious acts and say all of the flowery Christian talk they want. It doesn't mean that they are genuine. It may be that they know how to fake it really well. Nowhere is this more patently laid out in scripture than in the case of Judas.

In John 13, we have the account of Judas revealed as the betrayer. However, the response from the disciples along with the other accounts in Matthew and Luke make it clear that they didn't have a clue who it was at all. Only time will tell who are truly His and who are not. The Lord may reveal it while we are here on earth at which point we need to do what Jesus did to Judas: offer the gift of salvation and love and if they refuse, tell them to leave.

As I previously mentioned, not all who are in the church or profess to be a Christian are truly the Lord's. This distinction can be made by delineating the visible and the invisible church.

The Visible and Invisible Church

The visible church is the one we see in the world. It is made up of many who profess to be the Lord's or make the claim that they are the only true church. Full of contradiction and confusion at times, this is the church Christians identify with and the world sees. Another way of putting it is the visible church are the people who show up for a church gathering on Sunday and profess a belief in the Lord Jesus Christ.

The invisible church, on the other hand, is the true church. It is the church that God sees and knows and does not include everyone found in a pew on a Sunday morning. This differs from the Catholic view that believes that the visible church, namely the Catholic church, is the only true church.

It should be noted that the invisible church is almost always found among the visible church with some rare exceptions. There is no excuse for failing to fellowship with the saints of God regularly because it is an imperative from God to do so (Hebrews 10:25).

The hocus-pocus prayer of salvation that is so common in churches around the globe guarantees you nothing. We don't know every nuance of an individual's heart but we can inspect the fruit coming from a professing believer to see if it's lining up with their profession. Even then, it doesn't mean that at some future date that individual will not fall away from the faith and become apostate.

A pastor friend and I used to agree that just because someone professes a belief in Christ doesn't mean that their faith is genuine. If someone professed a belief in Christ, we weren't quick to say that the individual was now a Christian. Our response was summed up in two words. "We'll see."

17th century minister and Bible commentator, Matthew Henry, summed it up well when he said:

> Unfruitful professors are unfaithful professors; professors, and no more.[1]

Again, this is clearly seen in the case of the classic biblical apostate, Judas. Here was a man that ate, slept, walked, talked, and ministered with the Lord Jesus Christ. For three years, not only had he been in close proximity to the Lord but the disciples also. However, the Lord knew from the very beginning that he was never a true believer and stated as such:

Jesus answered them, Have not I chosen you twelve, and one of you is a devil? (John 6:70)

Judas was not the only one in scripture to depart from faith in God. King Saul and Jehosophat could be included along with Demas (2 Timothy 4:10), Diotrephes (3 John 9), and arguably Hymaneus (1 Timothy 1:20). This pattern, Paul stated, was going to be a part of the church dynamic:

*For I know this, that after my departing shall grievous wolves enter in among you, not sparing the flock. Also **of your own selves** shall men arise, speaking perverse things, to draw away disciples after them. (Acts 20:29-30)*

The church should be watchful and vigilant because the enemy is more dangerous when it arises from within. This doesn't mean that we are suspicious about everyone's salvation. That's not our job. But it is our job to make sure that those who are calling themselves Christians live up to that proclamation according to the scriptures. As Wayne Grudem puts it:

> ...the church should not tolerate in its membership "public unbelievers" who by profession or life clearly proclaim themselves to be outside the true church.[2]

This was the problem in the church of Pergamos and Thyratira in Revelation 2. Unbelievers had come in and infected the church causing the Lord to rebuke them, commanding them to repent and do something about it or He was going to do something about it . The purity of His church, His bride, is paramount. He is coming for a church without spot nor wrinkle (Ephesians 5:27). That means that sin must be dealt with whenever it rears its ugly head and purged from His church which includes those who do not belong (Matthew 22:11-13). In some cases, they may make themselves known as in the Revelation 2 passage, in which case the church is responsible to deal with it (1 Corinthians 5:4-7). In other cases, they may not become known at all until the Lord comes back and judges the earth (Matthew 13:24-30).

The Lord knows who are His and though there are bound to

be unbelievers in the church, we can rest assured that their charade will be found out, for the Lord declares:

Not every one that saith unto me, Lord, Lord, shall enter into the kingdom of heaven; but he that doeth the will of my Father which is in heaven. Many will say to me in that day, Lord, Lord, have we not prophesied in thy name? and in thy name have cast out devils? and in thy name done many wonderful works? And then will I profess unto them, I never knew you: depart from me, ye that work iniquity. (Matthew 7:21-23)

As His church, we do not need to exacerbate the problem by freely inviting and bringing them into the gathering that is only for the Lord's people. We don't need to add to the church's difficulties by allowing someone who neither has the right nor faculties to be a part of God's church. This is not a free-for-all. This is kingdom business for kingdom people.

Some people may say, "If we do what you say, there won't be anyone in the church." I beg to differ. Jesus Christ is the head of the church which means He'll take care of the details in terms of numerical growth. The apostles didn't come up with a five point plan to get people to join the church. They preached the gospel in the power of the Holy Spirit. We should do the same. We need to change our whole mindset from *going* to church to *being* the church. Numbers are not important. This is not about quantity and many times less is more.

When it comes to unbelievers, stop bringing them to church.

Start bringing them to Christ.

References

1. Matthew Henry, Matthew Henry Commentary on the Bible, John 15:2.

2. Wayne Grudem, Systematic Theology, pg. 857

Chapter 9

Just the FAQs Ma'am

THROUGHOUT THIS BOOK, I have presented a biblical argument that believers should stop bringing unbelievers to church gatherings. In the midst of all that's been said (and during the writing of this book), I expected there to be questions. In anticipation of that, I have compiled a list of Frequently Asked Questions and the answers to those questions which will hopefully clear up any confusion.

1. So if someone comes to your church you wouldn't let them in because they are an unbeliever?

If an unbeliever comes of their own volition to mine or anyone else's local church, then God has orchestrated it and we should be what God has called us to be as His children. That being said, I would be quick to explain the gospel to them so they would not believe that by simply showing up they were somehow a part of the true, invisible church of God. I would also make it clear that they were not a part of the fellowship until they had made a public confession and proclamation of fidelity to Christ at which time we as the body of Christ would hold them accountable to that proclamation.

I would also make it clear what they were allowed to do. They would not be allowed to join in communion. They would not be allowed to lead or join in prayer. They would not be allowed to comment on the teaching. They would be allowed to sit, watch, and listen.

This is quite different from me personally inviting and bringing them to the church knowing they are still in rebellion against God.

An exception to this would be if the church prayed and planned an evangelistic teaching geared towards calling the lost to repentance. But as mentioned, this would be an exception, not the norm.

2. How will they be saved if I don't bring them to church?

The church's job is not to be an evangelism factory where we bring in unbelievers and pop out a believer simply by showing up. The idea is not to bring them to church. The idea is to bring them to Christ. It is the job of all believers, individually, to spread the gospel and is wrapped up in the purpose of the church. So believers should spread the gospel and pray for the salvation of unbelievers within their sphere of influence so that those who would be saved would be revealed and added to the church. Believers need to know how to communicate the true gospel and share it at every opportunity.

3. What about all those people who became saved in a church service? Was that wrong to do that?

There's nothing wrong with unbelievers getting saved in a church gathering and it definitely does happen. But the church gathering is not for evangelism of unbelievers. I strongly disagree with the notion that every sermon needs to have a straight gospel message. I believe every sermon or teaching should have the word of God. That's enough.

The church gathering is for the people of God. So someone getting saved at a church gathering is not the rule but the exception as it was stated in Chapter 2. God's preferred way is for His people to go out into the world and spread the gospel wherever He has us.

There are ways to do things, better ways to do things, and the best ways to do things. Keeping to a biblical model in line with the word of God within the context of a proper understanding of the scriptures is always the best way of doing things for the church.

A friend of mine and proofreader of the book you are reading, Josh Niemi, made a comment on this that I thought was spot on. He said:

> God can strike a straight blow with a bent stick. But our job as believers is to follow the biblical pattern and leave the results to Him. Evangelism is successful whenever the Gospel is faithfully preached, because its purpose is not only to convert but to convict – the same sun that melts wax also hardens clay. In the end, pragmatism is not a legitimate excuse for an illegitimate action.

4. Are you saying it's a sin for me to bring people to church?

Well....yes and no.

God will overlook our ignorance at times to accomplish His will. But after He reveals His will to us, which is is the whole purpose of this book, He expects us to be obedient. When we realize what His word says and then don't do it, that's sin.

Also as was mentioned previously, doing so may lead to sin in the church. The road to hell is paved with good intentions.

5. In 1 Corinthians 14:23, Paul talks about unbelievers coming in among a church gathering. Doesn't that mean unbelievers are expected to be in the church?

No. Let's take a look at the passage closely.

First, Paul is giving a hypothetical situation which is different from one that's expected. If Paul was expecting unbelievers to normally be a part of the church, he wouldn't have said "if the whole church comes together" but "when the whole church comes together." The same in verse 24 when he states "if all prophesy" instead of "when all prophesy."

Second, this hypothetical was in relation to the gift of tongues being rightly utilized in the church gathering. It has nothing to do with the make up of the people of the church.

Third, the implication is that the unbeliever comes of their own volition, not because another Christian brought them.

On the other hand, the Lord and Paul warn us that there would be false converts among us and even the disciples had no clue that Judas was the one that was about to betray the Lord as was mentioned earlier. Simon Magus in Acts 8 is also an example. We should expect there to be unbelievers among us but we shouldn't make the problem worse by bringing them into the church when we know they have not made a confession of Jesus Christ as their Lord and a proclamation to obey Him.

6. Jesus said that Judas was a devil and yet He chose him as one of His disciples. Doesn't that prove that He accepts unbelievers in the church?

No, it doesn't.

The Lord Jesus did choose Judas as one of His disciples. As a matter of fact, it was by His sovereign decree that Judas betray Him so that the scriptures would be fulfilled (John 17:12). Judas was never a true disciple and the Lord knew He was not going to become a true disciple yet used His evil deed for the good of the world. This was not business as usual however, otherwise Paul would not have encouraged putting people out of the church who persisted in sin (1 Corinthians 5:1-5). It's also important to note that once Judas was revealed as a traitor and an unbelieving apostate, he was asked to leave.

However, most markedly is the fact that the church was not born yet, so using him as an example is not valid to the discussion of impenitent unbelievers being brought into the church by believers.

7. What about children? Are they also to be excluded from gathering with a church? Many of them don't understand what the gospel is.

There is a small nugget of truth to this but by and large I think the statement is erroneous and it sells our children short in the knowledge department which I think is an insult to their intelligence. They get a lot more than we think they do.

That being said, it is wholly appropriate and biblical to bring children to church.

Train up a child in the way he should go and when he is old, he will not depart from it. (Proverbs 22:6)

Until a child reaches an age where they are no longer under the authority of their parents and can make a volitional choice on whether or not the Lord will be their Lord, it is up to the parents to create an environment for the child where the Lord is worshiped. The church gathering helps in surrounding them with godly people and presenting a model to them of what should be a part of a true Christian's life.

Conclusion

It's All About the Word

I have sought to lay out the biblical precedent that we should stop bringing unbelievers to church and get back to the basics of bringing them to Christ. What I've presented has been validated by the scriptures themselves. This is not a new thing but a really old thing. It's because of the church's disobedience to the Word of God that we see the many problems that arise in the church today and I'm under no grand delusion that writing this book will make all of that disappear. Yet, I was compelled to write this book in light of the current time and culture we live in, understanding that it could be for any era. What I sought to accomplish was to encourage and exhort the people of God to get back to the plain teaching of the scriptures. My hope is that this book will add to the many that set the bar for us as God's people to truly be God's people according to His word without compromise.

As I mentioned earlier, I know that all of our woes won't be solved if we stop bringing unbelievers to church. But some of them will. I do know that if we stop bringing unbelievers to church and become more concerned with bringing them to Christ, we will have a transformation in the church universal that will reflect God's glory more than it does now. That is the ultimate encouragement of this book, that it would equip those who read it with a biblical foundation to spread the gospel and protect the sanctity of the church. We don't need to be an accessory to Satan who will be busy bringing in false converts and wolves from among his own. We are to fervently contend for the faith, unwavering in our proclamation of the truth and our love for one another as God's people. My hope is that this book has helped strengthen you in some way to do just that.

Thank you for your indulgence. May the Lord bless and keep you beloved.

Look for the next book in the *Stop the Madness* series:

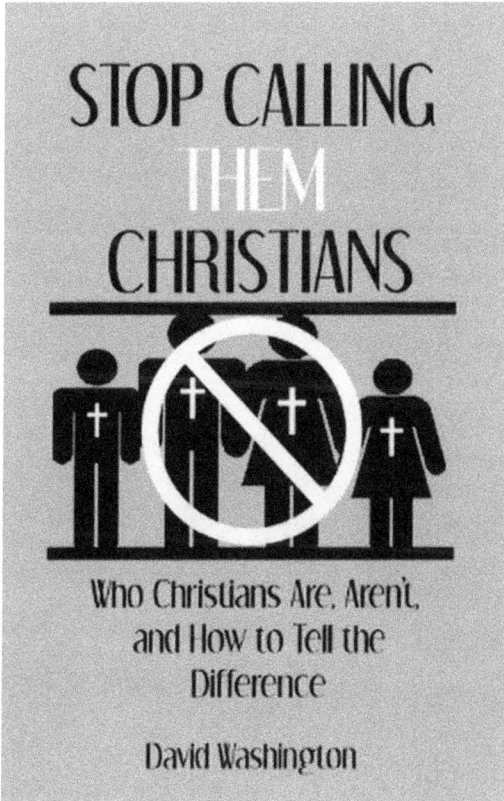

STOP CALLING
THEM
CHRISTIANS

Who Christians Are, Aren't,
and How to Tell the
Difference

David Washington

Summer 2014

You can also read more material at his church website,
Berean Home Fellowship at:
www.bereanhomechurch.org

Also, join David on his Facebook page at:

facebook.com/David.Washington.9083

www.ingramcontent.com/pod-product-compliance
Lightning Source LLC
Chambersburg PA
CBHW021153020426
42331CB00003B/40